JILL BRISCOE

VICTOR BOOKS®

A DIVISION OF SCRIPTURE PRESS PUBLICATIONS INC.
USA CANADA ENGLAND

Most Scripture quotations are taken from the *Holy Bible, New International Version* (NIV), © 1973, 1978, 1984, International Bible Society. Used by permission of Zondervan Bible Publishers. Other quotations are from the *King James Version* (KJV); *The Living Bible*, © 1971, Tyndale House Publishers, Wheaton, IL 60189. Used by permission; and from J.B. Phillips: *The New Testament in Modern English*, Revised Edition, © J.B. Phillips, 1958, 1960, 1972, permission of Macmillan Publishing Co. and Collins Publishers.

Recommended Dewey Decimal Classification: 248.4
Suggested Subject Heading: BIBLE STUDY—TOPICAL

Library of Congress Catalog Card Number: 87-81007
ISBN: 0-89693-319-9

VICTOR BOOKS
A division of SP Publications, Inc.
        Wheaton, Illinois 60187

·CONTENTS·

Recognition to Beth Donigan Seversen
for assistance
in researching and formulating
parts of this book.

•BEFORE YOU BEGIN•

People who gather together for Bible study are likely to be at different places in their spiritual lives, and their study materials should be flexible enough to meet their different needs. This book is designed to be used as a Bible study guide for such groups in homes or churches. It can also be used by individuals who are studying on their own. The lessons are written in five distinct sections, so that they can be used in a variety of situations. Groups and individuals alike can choose to use the elements they find most useful in the order they find most beneficial.

These studies will help you learn some new truths from the Bible as well as how to dig out those truths. You will learn not only *what* the Bible says, but how to use Scripture to deepen your relationship with Jesus Christ by obeying it and applying it in daily living. These studies will also provide an opportunity for potential leaders to learn how to lead a discussion in a nonthreatening setting.

What You'll Need

For each study you will need a Bible and this Bible study guide. You might also want to have a notebook in which to record your thoughts and discoveries from your personal study and group meetings. A notebook could also be used to record prayer requests from the group.

The Sections

Food for Thought. This is a devotional narrative that introduces the topic, person, or passage featured in the lesson. There are several ways it can be used. Each person could read it before coming to the group meeting, and someone could briefly summarize it at the beginning. It could be read silently by each person at the beginning of the session, or it could be read aloud, by one or several group members. (Suggested time: 10 minutes)

Talking It Over. This section contains discussion questions to help you review what you learn in Food for Thought. There are also questions to help you apply the narrative's truths to daily life. The person who leads the discussion of these questions need not be a trained or experienced teacher. All that is needed is someone to keep things moving and facilitate group interaction. (Suggested time: 30 minutes)

Praying It Through. This is a list of suggestions for prayer based on the lesson. You may want to use all the suggestions or eliminate some in order to leave more time for personal sharing and prayer requests. (Suggested time: 20 minutes)

Digging Deeper. The questions in this section are also related to the passage, topic, or character from the lesson. But they will not always be limited to the exact passage or character from Food for Thought. Passages and characters from both the Old and New Testaments will appear in this section, in order to show how God has worked through *all* of history in people's lives. These questions will require a little more thinking and some digging into Scripture, as well as some use of Bible study tools. Participants will be stretched as they become experienced in the "how-tos" of Bible study. (Suggested time: 45 minutes)

Tool Chest. The Tool Chest contains a description of a specific type of Bible study help and includes an explanation of how it is used. An example of the tool is given, and an example of it or excerpt from it is usually included in the Digging Deeper study.

The Bible study helps in the Tool Chest can be purchased by anyone who desires to build a basic library of Bible study reference books and other tools. They would also be good additions to a church library. Some are reasonably inexpensive, but others are quite expensive. A few may be available in your local library or in a seminary or college library. A group might decide to purchase one tool during each series and build a corporate tool chest for all the members of the group to use. You can never be too young a Christian to begin to master Bible study helps, nor can you be too old to learn new methods of rightly dividing the Word of truth.

The Tool Chest won't be used during the group time unless the leader wishes to draw special attention to it. Those who will be using the Digging Deeper study should read the Tool Chest on their own before or after doing the study.

6

Options for Group Use

Different groups, made up of people at diverse stages of spiritual growth, will want to use the elements in this book in different ways. Here are a few suggestions to get you started, but be creative and sensitive to your group's needs.

☐ Spend 5-15 minutes at the beginning of the group time introducing yourselves and having group members answer an icebreaker question. (Sample icebreaker questions are included under Tips for Leaders.)

☐ Extend the prayer time to include sharing of prayer requests, praise items, or things group members have learned recently in their times of personal Bible study.

☐ The leader could choose questions for discussion from the Digging Deeper section based on whether participants have prepared ahead of time or not.

☐ The entire group could break into smaller groups to allow different groups to use different sections. (The smaller groups could move to other rooms in the home or church where you are meeting.)

The key thing to remember is that you *don't have to feel obliged to use everything.* Pick what you or your group needs. Omit questions or reword them if you wish. Feel free to be flexible!

Tips for Leaders

Preparation

1. Pray for the Holy Spirit's guidance as you study, that you will be equipped to teach the lesson and make it appealing and applicable.

2. Read through the entire lesson and any Bible passages or verses that are mentioned. Answer all the questions.

3. Become familiar enough with the lesson that, if time in the group is running out, you know which questions could most easily be left out.

4. Gather all the items you will need for the study: name tags, extra pens, extra Bibles.

The Meeting

1. Start and end on time.

2. Have everyone wear a name tag until group members know one another's names.

3. Have each person introduce himself or herself, or ask regular attenders to introduce guests.

4. For each meeting, pick an icebreaker question or other activity

to help group members get to know one another better.

5. Use any good ideas to make everyone feel comfortable.

The Discussion

1. Ask the questions, but try to let the group answer. Don't be afraid of silence. Reword the question if it is unclear to the group or answer it yourself to clarify.

2. Encourage everyone to participate. If someone is shy, ask that person to answer an opinion question or other nonthreatening question. If someone tends to monopolize the discussion, thank that person for his or her contribution and ask if someone else has anything he or she would like to add. (Or ask that person to make the coffee!)

3. If someone gives an incorrect answer, don't bluntly or tactlessly tell him or her so. If it is partly right, reinforce that. Ask if anyone else has any thoughts on the subject. (Disagree agreeably!)

4. Avoid tangents. If someone is getting off the subject, ask that person how his or her point relates to the lesson.

5. Don't feel threatened if someone asks a question you can't answer. Tell the person you don't know but will find out before the next meeting—then be sure to find out! Or ask if someone would like to research and present the answer at the group's next meeting.

Icebreaker Questions

The purpose of these icebreaker questions is to help the people in your group get to know one another over the course of the study. The questions you use when your group members don't know one another very well should be very general and nonthreatening. As time goes on, your questions can become more focused and specific. Always give group members the option of passing if they think a question is too personal.

What do you like to do for fun?

What is your favorite season? dessert? book?

What would be your ideal vacation?

What exciting thing happened to you this week?

What was the most memorable thing you did with your family when you were a child?

What one word best describes the way you feel today?

Tell three things you are thankful for.

Imagine that your house is on fire. What three things would you try to take with you on your way out?

If you were granted one wish, what would it be?
What experience of your past would you most enjoy reliving?
What quality do you most appreciate in a friend?
What is your pet peeve?
What is something you are learning to do or trying to get better at?
What is your greatest hope?
What is your greatest fear?
What one thing would you like to change about yourself?
What has been the greatest accomplishment of your life?
What has been the greatest disappointment of your life?

Need More Help?

Here is a list of books that contain helpful information on leading discussions and working in groups:

How to Lead Small Group Bible Studies (NavPress, 1982).
Creative Bible Learning for Adults, Monroe Marlowe and Bobbie Reed (Regal, 1977).
Getting Together, Em Griffin (InterVarsity Press, 1982).
Good Things Come in Small Groups (InterVarsity Press, 1985).

One Last Thought

This book is a tool you can use whether you have one or one hundred people who want to study the Bible and whether you have one or no teachers. Don't wait for a brilliant Bible study leader to appear—most such leaders acquired their skills by starting with a book like this and learning as they went along. Torrey said, "The best way to begin, is to begin." Happy beginnings!

1
Presenting Our Bodies

•FOOD FOR THOUGHT•

"We spend only about twenty-five minutes a day in articulated speech. The rest of the time we communicate by waving, grimacing, grunting, frowning, shrugging, or long memos."[1] In other words, there are more ways to tell a husband you're mad at him than by chewing him out. Try being shrouded in silence, covered in prickles, or enjoying a pout—that will do it! Or have you ever watched a junior high kid when the preacher's gone overtime? Slumped in his seat, or head in hands, his body language says clearly, "I'm bored." Our bodies can communicate good messages too. The question is, what are our bodies saying to the world?

In Romans 12:1, the Apostle Paul says, "Therefore, I urge you, brothers, in view of God's mercy, to offer your bodies as living sacrifices, holy and pleasing to God—this is your spiritual act of worship." If we present our bodies to the Lord, He has the chance to use them as earthly vehicles of His divine action. And why should we do that? Paul gives us a reason—because of "God's mercy" (Rom. 12:1). It is because of the mercies of God that Jesus presented His body, as John 3:16 reminds us: "For God so loved the world that He gave His one and only Son." Jesus died, a living sacrifice for sinful man, so that we could go to heaven. What mercy! Close your eyes for a moment and try to picture the cross. What do you see? Jesus . . . with His arms outstretched to save, saying, "I love you." Now that's body language! Through His body, Jesus revealed the full extent of His redeeming love.

Seeing by His mercy that He did this for us, the least we can do is present our bodies back to Him. In the words of C.T. Studd, a famous pioneer missionary, "If Jesus Christ be God and died for me, then no sacrifice could be too great for me to make for Him!" C.T. Studd understood Romans 12:1.

Born of wealthy parents, C.T.'s father went to India to grow tea, later returning to England to enjoy the fruit of his labors. Not long afterward, D.L. Moody came to Britain and C.T.'s father went to Mr. Moody's meetings, heard him preach, and gave his life to the Lord. He then—in C.T.'s own words—gave "everyone in the house a dog's life of it until they were converted!" With the sudden death of his father, C.T. inherited incredible wealth. He enrolled as a student at Cambridge and played cricket for England. But he gave all that up to take the Gospel to those who had never heard—first to China, then to India, and finally to Africa. Observe his body language. His hands wrote the checks that transferred his huge wealth to charitable causes. His feet took him to three continents for Christ. His body, wracked with pain (they say a museum of diseases), bore in it the marks of his Lord. A body is—in my husband's words—"an earthly vehicle whereby a spiritual entity gets around in a physical environment." C.T.'s body sure got around!

We also see the principle of body language demonstrated in the life of the Apostle Paul. In Acts 8–9, we see Paul persecuting Christians. His mouth breathed out threats of slaughter (Acts 9:1). His feet chased the believers into hiding (8:1). And his hands dragged those who loved the Lord off to prison (9:2). But Saul, as he was then called, was converted on the road to Damascus. Immediately his body language changed. His feet took him to church (or to the synagogues, to be more precise). His mouth began proclaiming the good news about Jesus Christ. At the end of his incredible life, Paul was able to say, "I bear on my body the marks of Jesus" (Gal. 6:17). Paul found many ways to tell people he loved them for Jesus' sake!

So what is this body that I am to present? First of all, it is a *physical* entity. Paul placed a high premium on the body. The Greeks, however, thought that because the body did evil things, it must in itself be evil. This idea, of course, contradicts Scripture. From the very beginning the body has been an integral part of man's being. God dignified the body through creation, glorified it through the incarnation, and sanctifies the body through the work of His Holy Spirit. Though the "temple" of our flesh was desecrated through sin, salvation makes the difference. The body isn't evil. It is, simply, waiting for its full restoration in the resurrection (1 Cor. 15).

Romans 12:1 also reminds us that we are to *continually* present our bodies as a sacrifice. There is, undoubtedly, an element of cost involved. The very word *sacrifice* presupposes that. The problem I find personally in being a "living sacrifice" is that I keep crawling off the altar! Getting up early in the morning to do the housework in order to host a neighborhood Bible study can get old pretty quick when you have to do it every week. It all seems so glamorous and exciting at first and makes you feel good when you agree to do it, but when you've got three small children under school age who inevitably leave something of a Vietnam behind them in the living room, the physical cost of service is considerable. Oh, yes, crawling off the altar can be an alluring option for the young mom who is trying to be a *living* sacrifice!

In the early days of our marriage when my husband Stuart was away from home on missions business, how well I remember bathing and readying our three preschoolers for bed. Then I'd begin emptying our tiny living room, stacking the furniture in the garage in order to make room for several rows of chairs. After the baby-sitter arrived and had helped me move the larger pieces of furniture from the room, I would climb into our minivan and drive around the neighborhood, collecting as many ladies as I could persuade to come to our home for a Bible study. Occasionally I would return with only two ladies. "You did all that work for just two women?" you ask. Yes, because I never knew how many ladies would come; sometimes our little living room would cradle twenty-five precious women who wanted to learn more about Christ. Then after Bible study was over, I'd take the ladies back home, returning about midnight to unload the garage and clean up the kitchen. Only then could I drop into bed, praying the kids would sleep past six in the morning! That weekly meeting came around rather quickly—or so it seemed to me—and I learned to be a "living sacrifice," presenting not only a willing mind (to prepare the lesson), an open spirit (to say and practice what I preached), but also my physical service to God who I'd come to love because He first loved me!

To "present my body" means that it is *my* body I present, not someone else's. Not long ago, I heard a close relative of a missionary friend of mine say to her, "I think *you* should take care of your mother when she comes home from the hospital." That's called offering someone else's body, not your own!

Have you ever noticed how once you've professed to know Jesus Christ and have been bold enough to tell others whose you are and whom you serve, that some people will take advantage of you? Because you are the professedly "religious one" on the block, you may find yourself being volunteered for all sorts of good deeds that no one else wants to do. There will certainly be sacrifices you will be asked to make. But we must make sure that the sacrifices we are called on to make are the altars God has built specially for us.

Otherwise we could end up on someone else's privileged pyre, thereby robbing them of the joy of serving Jesus!

Something else we should notice about Romans 12:1 is that we are to offer God a body that is "holy" or "set apart from sin." This is the only kind of body that is acceptable to God. We do not offer our bodies to God in order to obtain salvation, of course. We offer our bodies to Him as a response of gratitude because He has obtained our salvation for us! This is—as Paul reminds us—a perfectly reasonable thing to do; it is our *reasonable* service. Other commentators translate this phrase, "spiritual act of worship." To worship and please God is the *least* I can do for Him because of the *most* He has done for me.

So, just how do I present this body of mine to God? And where do I present it? Do I take it to church, plant it in a pew, and leave it there? What does "presenting our bodies" mean in practical terms?

Presenting my body a holy, *continual* sacrifice is spiritual worship. The idea of continual tells me that spiritual worship can happen both inside and outside a church building. In other words, things like work—whether secular or sacred—can be an act of worship. Spiritual worship can also involve physical activity. The Christian life, after all, is not lived in a vacuum. We certainly need to enlist our minds and wills in spiritual worship. And we need to include our emotions too. But in the end, it is our bodies that are the agents of our spiritual ministry.

This exhortation to present our bodies is not just for the Pauls of this world either. Paul says, "I beseech *you*"—*you* being the little people, the ordinary Christians of the day, people like you and like me.

The morning I taught this particular Bible study, a plea was made for baby-sitters. Unfortunately the response from the women in the group was not very good. Later I overheard two ladies talking to each other.

"I love little children," gushed one of them.

The other lady, flashing her grandma pictures around, replied, "So do I!"

"Then I suggest you both present your bodies living sacrifices at the nursery room door," I chipped in with a grin. "They need help there!" They got the point. Knowing theology is one thing; practicing it another.

In the first eleven chapters of the Book of Romans, Paul is explaining the "mercies of God." But as chapter 12 begins we find him using the connecting word *therefore*, which reinforces the idea of the mercies of God being the overriding motivation for our service. If we never learn that Christianity has boots on, we are not likely to experience fully the joy of serving God. And if our boots of Christianity are not tied on with strings of grateful love, the march of faith will be a miserable experience indeed. "Therefore," says Paul, "I urge you, brothers, in view of God's mercy, to offer your bodies as living sacrifices, holy and pleasing to God—this is your spiritual act of worship. Do not conform any longer to the pattern of this world, but be transformed by the renewing of your mind. Then you will be able to test and approve what God's will is—His good, pleasing, and perfect will" (Rom. 12:1-2).

•TALKING IT OVER•

1. DISCUSS TOGETHER.   *8 minutes*
   ☐ What message is our modern American society
     giving us about our bodies?
   ☐ What are our bodies saying to our modern
     American society?
   ☐ What should our bodies be saying to our world?
   ☐ If you could choose one Scripture verse that
     talks about our bodies to share with someone
     who is not a believer, what verse would it be?
     Why?

2. READ AND DISCUSS IN TWOS.   *8 minutes*

   Psalm 139:16   Mark 5:29
   Proverbs 14:30   Luke 12:22-23
   Matthew 10:28   Romans 6:12

   ☐ Which verse teaches you something you didn't
     already know?
   ☐ Which verse do you most need to heed?
   ☐ Which verse seems impossible or difficult to
     experience?

3. BRAINSTORM AS A GROUP.   *10 minutes*
   Answer these questions: What is one way you
   could use your body this week as an act of spiritual
   worship or as your reasonable service to God?
   When will you do it? Pray about it together.

4. REFLECT INDIVIDUALLY.   *4 minutes*
   Ask yourself this question: What is my body saying
   to my world right now?

•PRAYING IT THROUGH•

Suggested Times

---

1. (On your own) Read Romans 12:1. Meditate on it. Then talk to God about it.

   5 minutes

---

2. (In twos) Isaiah 53 gives us a prophetic picture of Christ. Read this passage. Then praise the Lord for what you see of Christ's body language in this passage.

   5 minutes

---

3. (As a group) Pray for:
   ☐ Missionaries who are finding it tough to continually pay a "bodily price" for their faith.
   ☐ "Western" believers who at times seem to spend nothing at all for their faith.

   5 minutes

---

4. (On your own) Do the following:
   ☐ In prayer, present your body a living sacrifice to God. Is it a *holy* sacrifice? Talk to God about it.
   ☐ Praise Him for "accepting" the sacrifice you've offered. Remember, our sacrifices are to be "acceptable unto God."
   ☐ Pray about what your first "act" of reasonable service to God should be.

   5 minutes

•DIGGING DEEPER•

Romans 12:1

1. The word *therefore* in Romans 12:1 informs us that the writer, Paul, is making a transition, and that what he is about to say is logically linked to what he has just said.

   Skim the immediate context of Romans 12, which is chapter 11, and answer this question: In light of Paul's statement—"Therefore . . . in view of God's mercy"—what reasons has Paul previously given for what is to follow?

2. In what ways has God shown Himself merciful in your life?

3. Before Paul exhorts his readers to take action ("offer your bodies"), he reminds them *why* they should comply with his request ("God's mercy"). As Christians, what ought to be our motivation for obeying God's commands?

4. People obey God for a variety of reasons, some of which are wrong. Try to recall a situation in the past when you obeyed for the wrong reason.

   By what are you prone to be motivated?

5. Knowing what you do now about what our motivation as Christians should be, how will you respond to God's direction this week?

6. Describe the mood and force behind Paul's words in Romans 12:1-2.

7. The word *urge* (*parakaleō* in the Greek) has three shades of meaning: (1) to beseech in the sense of an invitation or a request; (2) to exhort by an authoritative appeal; (3) to comfort.[2]

   Using a concordance, and following the steps outlined in the Tool Chest section of this chapter, do a word study of *urge* (*parakaleō*) to determine which nuance of the word makes the most sense as it is used in Romans 12:1. (You will find it helpful to look up other words such as *entreat, exhort,* and *beseech.*) Do this exercise on your own paper.

   Once you have completed this exercise, check your findings against your answer to question #6 in this study. Did you accurately identify Paul's mood and force the first time?

8. Why do you suppose Paul was not more specific with his readers about what they were to offer God?

   What could we possibly offer God that would begin to compare with His mercy toward us?

   Is there an area of your life which you have not yet been able to completely surrender to the Lord? What is it?

9. Another reason for offering ourselves completely to God is that we belong to Him. What two prominent doctrinal themes in Scripture teach that we belong to God? (cf. Rom. 5:1-11; Rom. 11:36; 1:25)

   If we are not our own, but are God's possession, then we have no rights of our own. What rights have you not yet surrendered to

Him? (Example: privacy, cleanliness, friendships, financial stability, work)

10. According to Romans 12:1, what constitutes true Christian worship?

What does John 4:23-24 add to your understanding of true worship?

Is worship in your life confined to a Sunday morning church service?

What connection do you see between Sunday worship services and spiritual worship, which is to encompass the whole of a believer's life?

Complete this sentence: Worship is unacceptable to God when . . .

11. What practical difference will Romans 12:1 make in your life this week?

Write a prayer request for yourself on the basis of what you have learned from this study.

For Further Study
1. Read Romans 1–11 this week. As you read, list all the mercies of God you observe in these chapters of which Paul's *therefore* would have reminded his readers.
2. Study the word *offering* or *sacrifice* in a Bible dictionary or handbook and record your findings.
3. Memorize Romans 12:1.

•TOOL CHEST•
(A Suggested Optional Resource)

WORD STUDIES
Just as words in the English language many times have more than one meaning, so do words in the languages of Scripture. A word study can help you isolate the specific meaning of a word in relation to its other usages. Use the simple four-step approach which follows to do a word study.

STEP 1: Choose a word that is difficult to understand, unusual, or of special interest to you and look it up in an exhaustive Bible concordance. Examine all or many of the word's occurrences in the Bible, making sure you look at each verse within its given context. Write down a brief definition for every occurrence of the word.

STEP 2: Group your findings into several categories. Each category should define a different shade of meaning of the word. The following excerpt from an English dictionary serves as an example. Notice the seven categories.

> **fac•ul•ty** / făk'-el-tē / *n., pl.* -ties. **1:** An inherent power or ability. **2:** Any of the powers or capacities possessed by the human mind. **3:** The ability to perform well in a given activity; skill. **4:** *Obsolete.* Occupation; trade. **5:** *Abbr.* fac. *Education.* **a:** Any of the divisions or comprehensive branches of learning at a college or university: *the faculty of law.* **b:** The instructors with such a division. **c:** Any body of teachers as distinguished from their students. **6:** All of the members of a learned profession: *the medical faculty.* **7:** Authorization granted by authority; conferred power.[3]

STEP 3: Determine what the basic idea or common thread is among all occurrences of the word. There will be one element in common to all its usages.

STEP 4: Decide which category the verse you've just looked up best fits into and note how that specific nuance relates to the basic meaning of the word.

Complete the following word study for the Hebrew word חָפֵר, which is transliterated *chapher* (Hebrew).

STEP 1: Look up all or many of the occurrences of the word in Scripture.

Reference   Context

Job 6:20

Ps. 34:5

Ps. 35:4

Ps. 35:26

Ps. 40:14

Ps. 70:2

Ps. 71:24

Ps. 83:17

Prov. 13:5

Prov. 19:26

Isa. 1:29

Isa. 24:23

Isa. 41:11

Isa. 54:4

Jer. 15:9

Jer. 50:12

STEP 2: Group your findings into categories.

a. to be ashamed	b. to shame; reproach	c. to be con- fused
references:	references:	references:
————————	————————	————————
————————	————————	————————
————————	————————	————————
————————	————————	————————
————————	————————	————————
————————	————————	————————

STEP 3: State the basic idea.

STEP 4: Answer these questions:

What does *chapher* mean in Micah 3:7?

What is its relationship to the basic meaning of all its usages?

A word study helps us learn the precise meaning of a word in a particular passage of Scripture. Once you have completed a few word studies on your own, you may find the exercise so enjoyable you will decide to write your own Bible dictionary!

On a tight budget? A compact concordance is not outside your reach. This particular type of concordance is limited in that it does not list every occurrence of a word, but usually it does give the most significant ones. *Cruden's Compact Concordance*

(Zondervan) is one helpful, less expensive volume of this type. Also, a good Bible will contain a concordance, which may be just as useful as a compact concordance.

Why not ask for an exhaustive concordance for your birthday or Christmas? Here are just a few to choose from:

Concordances for *King James Version* Bibles:
Strong's Exhaustive Concordance of the Bible (Abingdon)
Young's Analytical Concordance to the Bible (Eerdmans)

Concordance for the *New International Version:*
The NIV Complete Concordance (Zondervan)

Concordance for the *New American Standard Bible:*
New American Standard Exhaustive Concordance (Holman)

Concordance for the *Revised Standard Version:*
Nelson's Complete Concordance to the Revised Standard Version (Nelson)

2

Transforming Our Minds

•FOOD FOR THOUGHT•

"Don't let the world around you squeeze you into its mold, but let God remake you so that your whole attitude of mind is changed" (Rom. 12:2). What we think, we are! In other words, the quality of our lives is closely related to the quality of our thinking, and the quality of our thinking is interpreted through our body actions. The body does not act independently of the instructions it receives from the mind, so who or whatever is directing my life will determine my body language.

If giving my body to God as a living sacrifice is the *reasonable* thing to do (Rom. 12:1), then it stands to reason that to withhold myself from God's direction is an *unreasonable* thing to do!

In church circles today we hear a lot about the "fashion of this age," and what we're told is that we must reject it. So what *is* the pattern of this world out of which is cut the fashion of this age? *World* or *age* refers to the spiritual state of things, not to its material state; it means the "spirit of the age" or "the world's standards." And it is this spirit we must resist. The Apostle John warns us to neither adopt, imitate, or love these worldly standards (1 John 2:15).

My husband Stuart interprets "the lust of the flesh, the lust of the eyes, and the pride of life" (1 John 2:16) as *passions, possessions,* and *position.* These words, I'm sure you will agree, are an apt description of the spirit of our age.

Think for a moment about what is happening all around us. The "lust of the flesh" is seen in the plethora of skin magazines and growing soft porn market that saturate our society today. "Why," you may ask, "does the church need to hold conferences to address the issue of pornography?" Because the "fashion of this world" would mold our minds after its own, perverting God's concept of sex and love. *Eros* reigns; *agape* is ridiculed.

Then there is the matter of the "lust of the eyes"—*possessions.* Greed translated is "what people see, they want." To see something is to want it, and to want it is to buy it whether it is affordable or not!

Finally, there is the "pride of life"—*position.* A man who is thinking "the world's thoughts" takes great pride in considering himself supreme and unrivaled in his own self-importance. It is not surprising that ours has been called the "me" generation.

Narcissism takes its name from the mythical god, Narcissus, who fell in love with his own reflection in a pool. Someone sent me an astute piece of humor by Erma Bombeck who sums up the spirit of our age:

> During the last year I have dissected my marriage, examined my motives for buying, interpreted my fantasies, come to grips with mid-life, found inner peace, outer flab, charted my astrological stars, become my best and only friend. I have brought order to my life, meditated, given up guilt, adjusted to the new morality, and spent every living hour understanding me, interpreting me, and loving me. And—you know what? I am bored to death of me!'

The transient temptations we face over transient things will leave us with transient experiences, resulting in disillusionment and despair. Such pursuits should send us off in search of the permanent!

John reminds us that "the world and all its possessions and desires will one day disappear, but the man who is following God's will is part of the *permanent* and *lives forever*" (1 John 2:17).

The problem is, there is a spirit of this age that would win the battle for our minds. He would have us believe that we ourselves are gods. That we will never die. That we owe it to ourselves to pay homage to so splendid a creature. He has so blinded our minds with "self" that we cannot see our true condition, nor can we see our Saviour. He would even have us believe that his flashy neon lights will illuminate our souls to see the world the way it *really* is. He wants us to believe that the True Light blinds us to reality. That we live in a fool's paradise, oblivious to all the fun there is to be had. More than once I've been told, "You Christians don't know what it is to *really* live!" How often I find myself needing to pray the words of this favorite hymn of mine:

> Oh, let me feel Thee near me,
> The world is ever near;

I see the sights that dazzle,
The tempting sounds I hear:
My foes are ever near me,
Around me and within;
But, Jesus, draw Thou nearer,
And shield my soul from sin.²

We must not be conformed to this world. Instead, we are to be *transformed* (Rom. 12:2). The word used here (v. 2) is an interesting one. It means "to change the external form because an internal change has taken place." It implies spiritual transformation. In fact, the same word is used to describe Jesus' *transfiguration*—a transformation so obvious that everyone who was there could not help but see the change. In English, the Greek word for *transformed* is translated *metamorphosis*. According to Webster, metamorphosis is "a striking alteration in appearance, character, or circumstances."

Cocoons and bugs and butterflies come to mind when we think of metamorphosis. We have a choice of leaving our worldly cocoon behind and flying into God's free world.

Wouldn't it be lovely if a bug could stay always
Warm inside its silk cocoon, protected all its days
Alone in dark oblivion, no need to fly the skies?
Let's face it—God's rebellious world's no place for
    butterflies.

Now God, He made these little bugs and placed
    within *His life*
So growth, the natural evidence, brings strain and
    stress and strife;
For as she grows the cozy case becomes a prison
    strong,
The bug now knows she *must* break out; to stay a
    bug is *wrong.*

At last the struggle over—the butterfly is free
    to fly God's earth upheld by Him in matchless
    symmetry.
Cries watching man in God's world, "*A miracle
    is this,*
From crumpled bug to butterfly"—
                    *God's metamorphosis.*³

So how does this marvelous spiritual transformation take place? "By the renewing of our minds." That will never happen, of course, unless our minds are informed. Reformation requires information. In his book _The Magnificent Mind_, Gary Collins tells us that the mind is the man; the brain his computer. He says that the mind and the brain do not operate on quite the same principle. The brain, for instance, can lose as many as 100,000 cells a day—cells which are never replaced. Yet when we reach a ripe old age, our brains can still function well. This is because we have more brain cells than there are stars in the sky! But our computer brain can go "wrong." It can only put out what is put into it. Our _minds_, on the other hand, have been linked to the soul. It is the mind that is able to appreciate the moral of a story, the punch line of a joke, or can make a moral choice. The mind needs transfiguring. It needs changing. It needs God's metamorphosis.

The "renewed mind" is one that has been touched by the Holy Spirit, who, using the Word of God, informs it of correct ways to think about the Lord, ourselves, and our world. As we expose ourselves to the Scriptures on an ongoing basis and allow God's Spirit to interpret them to us, we are led to repentance and regeneration, which leads to a new way of thinking. Then we are able to "prove"— examine and spiritually scrutinize—God's will for ourselves. We will find ourselves believing that His will is absolutely good and perfect, lacking nothing. What is more, we discover that God's will is not only perfect, it is acceptable!

This does not mean that a transformed mind will always understand what is happening, or how unacceptable circumstances can become acceptable. What it does mean is that the person who possesses a renewed mind will be able to understand what must be done in the complex and painful issues of life. He _will_ find the necessary power to do what is right midst difficult circumstances. And he will also be able to submit to the secret council of God, allowing Him to explain the "unexplainable" if and when He will!

The fact that God has a plan for each of our lives should bring order to our souls; His eternal purposes are being worked out. The wonder of all this is that in the middle of His inscrutable divine plans, He takes _us_ into consideration—thinking of us, blessing us, using us, helping us, and healing us.

Not long ago, I was faced with a difficult decision concerning my teaching ministry. Personal health problems were making it next to impossible to travel as much as I had hoped. This problem became a complex and painful issue of life for me. I asked God to renew my mind and help me to submit to the secret council of His will regarding *my* future plans. As I yielded to God my demand to see the whole game plan, and asked for only the power and courage to play the next play—leaving the unknown out of the game—I knew what to do. Doing God's will then became a matter of obedience. I tried to live day by day—testing, scrutinizing, and examining events, advice, and the Word of God in order to keep in line with what I discerned to be God's will for my life.

What I discovered was that I needed to stop asking, "Why has this happened?" and start asking, "What must I do today?" adding, "and You look after tomorrow!" Jesus Himself said, "Sufficient unto the day is the evil thereof; therefore, take no thought for tomorrow" (Matt. 6:34).

Accepting God's will for today means refusing to accept tomorrow until it comes. And doing that takes a conscious act of the will, as I'm fast discovering! It also transforms my todays and helps me concentrate on making every present moment count!

•TALKING IT OVER•

1. EVALUATE AND SHARE.   *7 minutes*
   ☐ If you were to describe your state of mind right
   now, which of the following words would you
   use? (Circle one.)

   Conformed   Transformed   Informed

   ☐ What is one thing you have learned today about
   transforming your mind that will help you?

2. READ AND RESPOND.   *8 minutes*
   ☐ Think of a bad situation in your life right now.
   Then read Philippians 4:8 and think some "Phi-
   lippians 4:8" thoughts about that situation.
   ☐ Write a sentence describing one good thing
   about your present circumstances and thank
   God for what you will learn about God, your-
   self, and others through it.

3. READ AND DISCUSS.   *15 minutes*
   As a group, read Psalm 42. Then discuss these
   questions:
   ☐ What would you say is the psalmist's state of
   mind as he is writing this psalm?
   ☐ Why is his state of mind what it is? (v. 9)
   ☐ Which verses specifically talk about the psalm-
   ist's mind-set?
   ☐ What can we learn from this psalm that will help
   us keep a right attitude this week?

•PRAYING IT THROUGH•

1. (On your own) Silently think about God for a moment. Surrender your thoughts to Him. Then read Romans 12:1-2, praying through these verses thought by thought.

2 minutes

2. (As a group) Pray for:
   □ Those you know who have conformed to the thinking of this world. Pray that their minds would be *transformed* and *informed*.
   □ Each other, that each of you would learn to think your thoughts after God's thoughts.
   □ Your children and loved ones, that the Holy Spirit would win the battle for their minds.

5 minutes

3. (In twos) Complete the following:
   □ Choose a story about Jesus from one of the Gospels and read it together.
   □ Think about it. How was Jesus living a Romans 12:1-2 life?
   □ Pray that you will be more like Jesus.

   (On your own) Spend time:
   □ Asking God to transform your mind so that you can accept His will for you.
   □ Talking with God about tomorrow. Can you leave your tomorrow in His hands?

10 minutes

4. (As a group) Praise God for all the things your minds have been thinking about in the stories you have just read.

3 minutes

•DIGGING DEEPER•

Romans 12:2

1. Are the instructions which are given in Romans 12:2 optional for a Christian? Why or why not?

2. Look up the word *conform* in a dictionary and record its meaning below.

   What are some "patterns of this world" you participated in before becoming a believer in Christ?

3. Can you think of some popular slogans, quips, or jingles that focus on patterns of thinking that are wrong and which Christians should avoid? List any that come to mind below.

   Now read through Romans 12:3-21 and come up with a list of "patterns of this world" to which Paul alludes and to which believers are not to comply.

4. Is Paul speaking of a particular event or a process when he commands us to "be transformed"? (v. 2) What support can you give for your answer based on the given context of this phrase?

5. What do you think it means to "renew your mind"? (v. 2)

   What are some areas of your mind that need renewing? (Examples: desires, fantasies, mental pictures, fears, etc.)

6. What are some pure and positive thoughts, Scripture verses, or good memories you could concentrate on next time you find yourself thinking about something about which you should *not* be thinking?

7. To "test and approve what God's will is" means "to understand what He expects and desires from us." From your study of this chapter, what do you know—beyond a shadow of a doubt—God's expressed will to be for your life?

8. What *one* aspect of this world's thinking are you in conformity with that must stop?

   Name *one* step you ought to take to renew your mind.

9. Pray that God will enable you, by His Holy Spirit, to make the needed transformation in your life.

•TOOL CHEST•
(A Suggested Optional Resource)

INTERLINEAR GREEK-ENGLISH NEW TESTAMENT

A Greek-English interlinear makes available to Bible students a word-for-word translation of the New Testament. The Greek text is provided and underneath it is printed the English translation. Romans 12:1-2 from the *New International Version Interlinear Greek-English New Testament* is shown below.[4]

THEREFORE, I urge you, brothers, in view of God's mercy, to offer yourselves as living sacrifices, holy and pleasing to God—which is your spiritual worship. [2]Do not conform any longer to the pattern of this world, but be transformed by the renewing of your mind. Then you will be able to test and approve what God's will is—his good, pleasing and perfect will.

12 Παρακαλῶ οὖν ὑμᾶς, ἀδελφοί, διὰ
    I beseech therefore you,   brothers, through

τῶν οἰκτιρμῶν τοῦ θεοῦ, παραστῆσαι τὰ
the compassions   –   of God, to present   the

σώματα ὑμῶν θυσίαν ζῶσαν ἁγίαν τῷ
bodies of you sacrifice a living   holy   –

θεῷ εὐάρεστον, τὴν λογικὴν λατρείαν
[a]to God [1]well-pleasing, the reasonable   service

ὑμῶν· 2 καὶ μὴ συσχηματίζεσθε τῷ αἰῶνι
of you;   and   be ye not conformed   age

τούτῳ, ἀλλὰ μεταμορφοῦσθε τῇ ἀνακαινώσει
to this,   but   be ye transformed by, the   renewing

τοῦ νοός, εἰς τὸ δοκιμάζειν ὑμᾶς τί τὸ
of the mind, *for* *the* to prove   you[b] what the
                   =so that ye may prove

θέλημα τοῦ θεοῦ, τὸ ἀγαθὸν καὶ εὐάρεστον
will   – of God, the   good   and well-pleasing

καὶ τέλειον.
and   perfect.

A study tool of this type can be a very helpful resource, especially when reading a critical commentary. (Critical commentaries focus on the technical aspects of the text rather than on the theological aspects.) A critical commentary often gives the Greek word and a definition, but omits the English equivalent of the word. In such an instance, one can use his/her interlinear Bible to locate the Greek word in the verse he/she is studying. Below it you will find the English translation of the word.

Some interlinear New Testaments are based on personal translations of the Greek, while others are based on a particular translation such as the *New International Version*.

The Interlinear Greek-English New Testament (Zondervan)
The NASB Interlinear Greek-English New Testament (Zondervan)
The RSV Interlinear Greek, New Testament (Zondervan)

3

Changing Our Hearts

•FOOD FOR THOUGHT•

On one occasion a sharp, young Sadducee asked Jesus, "Of all the commandments, which is the most important?" (Mark 12:28) Our Lord was being questioned, or rather "baited" before an ever-critical crowd of religious leaders. In a very straightforward manner, Jesus made it clear to the young man that to "love the Lord your God with all your heart and with all your soul and with all your mind and with all your strength" is the most important commandment of all (Mark 12:28). In our passage for this study (Luke 10:25-37), we see these words repeated and Jesus illustrating His point with the story of the good Samaritan.

The Lord knew that orthodox Jews recited these words (Luke 10:27) they called the "Shema" every morning and evening. (It is the Jewish confession of faith.) Jesus wanted to link the principle of this command to Leviticus 19:18, where God reminds His people that loving one's neighbor is to be the natural outgrowth of loving God.

The Hebrews believed that the heart was the central organ of the body and, therefore, was the very center of a man's moral, spiritual, and intellectual life. They also believed it to be the seat of a man's emotions, passions, and appetites. *Heart* was the term used to describe the place where our most meaningful experiences and relationships take place.

Today, we continue to use the word *heart* in the same way. The story is told of a preacher who once faced a heckler who was ridiculing the idea of "Christ living in the heart." Having just passed a butcher's shop, the man had seen a heart hanging on a hook, and he quickly reminded the preacher that the heart is just a blood pump. The preacher asked the man if he had ever done any "courting," then simply observed that he was quite sure the gentleman had never gazed into his beloved's eyes and stated, "Darling, I love you with all my blood pump!" The preacher's point was well taken. So then, how *do* we love God with *all* our hearts as we are commanded to?

Every one of us is born with a serious heart defect known as sin (Rom. 5:12-14). Man looks on the outside, but God—with X-ray-like eyes—looks on the inside (1 Sam. 16:7). And He sees the heart of man and knows it is continually evil. His divine diagnosis is sobering: "The heart is deceitful above all things and beyond cure" (Jer. 17:9). The Word of God gives us a very serious prognosis. It describes the heart as "wicked, perverse, and the seat of sin," and it pictures the heart as resisting God and defiling the whole man. Jesus, in effect, is saying that the heart affects everything—"For out of the heart come evil thoughts, murder, adultery, sexual immorality, theft, false testimony, slander" (Matt. 15:19).

Even spiritual bypass surgery will not correct the terrible ravages caused by sin in the human heart. Nothing less than a transplant will do! The message Jesus came to deliver, however, is that God has promised man such a transplant: "I will give you a new heart and put a new spirit in you; I will remove from you your heart of stone and give you a heart of flesh" (Ezek. 36:26).

God had also found a donor. There was only one problem—the donor was still alive. The "heart" of the Gospel is an operating table in the shape of a cross, a willing donor—Jesus Christ, God's only Son, and the incredible offer of His heart and mind in place of our diseased ones. We can receive the heart of God Himself to replace our own hearts of stone. The Holy Spirit is the divine Surgeon who will fix our hearts in such a way that they can never be rejected. All this, however, depends on our agreeing to the operation. It is a decision which should not be taken lightly as it will have eternal repercussions.

Once in place, we find that our new hearts beat with love for lost mankind. With valves wide open, and as grateful recipients of new life, we cannot help but actively look for men and women who have fallen into the ditch as they've traveled along the highways and byways of life.

"So, I am to love my neighbor as myself, am I?" the young expert in the Law demanded of Jesus. "And just who *is* my neighbor?"

Jesus answered him simply, "The man in the ditch."

"And who is that?" you ask. It is the girl robbed of her husband by another woman. The child robbed of her mother by her mother's boss. The college kid robbed of his opportunity by the recession. The teenager robbed of her virginity by her high school date. The person in the ditch might also be the woman robbed of her reputation by malicious gossip or the elderly person robbed of his health by disease. There are plenty of people in the ditch, but never enough good Samaritans to go around.

So *how* are we to love these "people in the ditch"? As we love ourselves. Implicit in our Lord's answer is permission to think rightly (with acceptance) about ourselves. To love and care for the person in the ditch is to do as much for that person as you would do for yourself. In other words, ask yourself, "If I were lying in a ditch bleeding to death, what would I do for me?" Then you will know what to do.

Of course, there is always a risk involved in doing things for strangers. And there will be plenty of "robbers" around to steal from you the joy of serving the needy. But if you never live on risk's edge, you'll never depend on God. And if you never depend on God, you'll never grow as a loving person. Yes, there is a risk in loving others who may not be able to love you in return, but it must be done. The new heart within you demands it. The very heart concern of God Himself should become your heart concern, lending you the compassion to care, and enabling you to go where the need is (Luke 10:33). You will find yourself actively getting alongside those in despair, putting your arms around them, and lifting them out of trouble.

The good Samaritan was willing to put out for the man—bandaging his wounds, pouring on oil and wine, placing him on his own donkey while he walked alongside, and paying for his room in an inn. The Samaritan's love was demonstrated practically. But then, isn't that what loving God is all about? As Spurgeon once said, "If you want to give a man a tract, wrap it in a sandwich." My own experience beautifully illustrates the truth of these things.

I was converted to Christ while in college. Until I reached the point where I recognized I needed to know God through Christ, I have to confess that my heart was purely selfish. I had no concern for anyone else, unless, of course, they fit into my scheme of things and could be used to accomplish my own ends. Then came conversion! Christ removed my stony, hardhearted attitude and gave me a heart of flesh. Practically speaking, this conversion resulted in my developing a concern for underprivileged people. Not only was this a totally new experience of loving others more than myself, it also led to an involvement in full-time ministry. Every part of life was affected— my time, my finances, my ambitions, even the choice of my life partner. Of this you can be certain—when God gives you His heart, you will begin to love those He loves in the way He loves them and life will never be the same again.

So when am I to begin loving God with all my heart? The very moment He gives me Himself. And when should I begin loving others as myself? Today—in the ordinary course of daily affairs; when I'm on my way from Jerusalem to Jericho; whenever I see a man in a ditch. I must not be like the priest who was too busy running to Bible study to help, or like the Levite who didn't consider it *his* responsibility to turn aside to see what he could do. No, I am to be like the good Samaritan who loved in deed and truth. With this God will surely be pleased!

•TALKING IT OVER•

1. SHARE TOGETHER.   *10 minutes*
   (To be completed in groups of 6 to 8 people each.)

   Have you had a spiritual heart transplant? What difference has it made in your life? (Share your experiences with each other.)

2. READ AND DISCUSS.   *10 minutes*
   Read Luke 10:25-37 and discuss the questions which follow.
   ☐ Share a time when you were a good Samaritan to someone else, or an incident when someone helped you when you were in a "ditch." What impact did this experience have on your life?
   ☐ Who do you think the priest and the Levite in this parable represent?
   ☐ Have you, like the priest and Levite, ever passed by on the other side? Why?

3. REFLECT.
   ☐ (God's family) As a group, read Romans 12:9-   *5 minutes*
   21. Then share with one another the verses that speak most clearly to you, putting them into your own words.

   ☐ (My family) At the moment, who do you find it   *5 minutes*
   hardest to love? (Circle one.)

   Mother   Father   Child

   Grandparent   In-law   Sister   Brother

   ☐ Write down one thing you've learned today that will make a difference in your life.

•PRAYING IT THROUGH•

*Suggested
Times*

1. (Corporately or in twos) Praise God for:
   □ Providing a "spiritual heart transplant" for you.
   □ Providing people for you to love.
   □ Providing people to love you.
   □ Christians who have shown you specific acts of love.

5 minutes

2. (Corporately) Pray for people in the ditch—those at work, your neighbors, your church, your community, and the world.

10 minutes

3. (Silently) Ponder and pray.
   □ Who is the man, woman, or child in the "ditch" that you can love?
   □ Pray that God would make you willing to love that person practically, and that you would know what action needs to be taken to do just that.
   □ (In twos) Share with your prayer partner what God has impressed on you to do. Then do it!

5 minutes

•DIGGING DEEPER•

1. In Scripture, King David alone is acclaimed as "a man after God's own heart" (1 Sam. 13:4; Acts 13:22). King Saul's heart, on the other hand, eventually rotted away as he turned from the Lord to a life of perversity, corruption, and every other imaginable selfishness.

   Read 1 Samuel 13:1-15 and note in the space below the characteristics of "a heart after self" versus those of "a heart after God."

   A Heart after God   A Heart after Self

2. (Self-examination) Does your heart reflect the attitudes and motives of Saul or David? Identify both the positive and negative desires of your own heart.

   Positive Desires   Negative Desires

   What selfish choices have you made in the last week which may reveal that you have a wrong heart condition?

   Take a moment right now to confess your sin to the Lord and ask Him to both cleanse and purify your heart. Then thank Him for His *unfailing love*.

3. When Samuel was sent to anoint David as King of Israel, He mistook David's brother Eliab, for the Lord's anointed (1 Sam. 16:6). The Lord redirected the prophet with these words, "Do not consider his appearance or his height, for I have rejected him. The Lord does not look at the things man looks at. Man looks at the outward appearance, but the Lord looks at the heart" (1 Sam. 16:7). Which did you give more attention to this morning, your appearance or your heart?

Imagine the Lord peering into your heart today. What would He see?

What do you suppose the Lord saw in David's heart that would move Him to anoint David king over all Israel?

4. While yet a young man, anointed but uncrowned, how did the condition of David's heart affect his response in the following situations?

1 Samuel 17:25-58

1 Samuel 21:10-15

5. Years later, the crowned and celebrated king exhibited a fickle heart. Read the account in 2 Samuel 11 of David's miserable failure before the Lord.

What was David's first downward step toward a time in his life which was characterized by personal tragedy and destruction?

Trace his ensuing steps down the slippery slope of willful disobedience. Pinpoint each selfish decision.

6. If you had been a close friend of David's, what would you have said to him to try to prevent him from falling into sin?

When someone who is close to you tries to encourage you or warn you with scriptural principles and advice, what is your reaction and/or response?

7. At different times in their lives, both Saul and David displeased the Lord. How is it that David's house and kingdom were established by the Lord and Saul's weren't? Why would the Lord promise David, not Saul, "But My love will never be taken away from him, as I took it away from Saul, whom I removed from before you. Your house and your kingdom will endure forever before Me; your throne will be established forever"? (2 Sam. 7:15-16)

Why do you think a holy and just God promised to do this for a murderer?

8. Psalm 51 is believed to be an outpouring of David's heart to the Lord after he was convicted about his acts of adultery and murder. How is David's heart depicted in this psalm?

Rethink your answers to question #7. Write down below any additional thoughts you may have.

9. God used the Prophet Nathan to confront David about his disobedience. Who are the "Nathans" in your life the Lord has used as instruments of His love and grace?

Recall a time when you committed a sin that left you feeling devastated. How did you respond when the Holy Spirit convicted you of the wrongness and the gravity of your transgression? Was it similar to David's?

REMEMBER: Next time the Holy Spirit convicts you of a sin in your life, stop right then and repent of your disobedience, humbly asking your Heavenly Father to forgive you.

10. From the perspective of Psalm 51, what do you think God saw in David's heart?

What would you like God to see in your heart today?

11. Prayerfully reread Psalm 51, confessing your own faults to the Lord as you read. Take comfort in the fact that God willingly blessed and used David for His own purposes and glory despite David's disobedience.

12. List the lessons you have learned from King David's life and character.

In his character study of David's life, F.B. Meyer records this lesson, which we should take to heart.

Sin is dark, dangerous, damnable; but it cannot stanch the love of God; it cannot change the love that is not of yesterday, but dates from eternity itself. The only thing that can really hurt the soul is to keep its confession pent within itself. If only with stuttering, broken utterance it dares to cry, "Be merciful to me, the sinner, for the sake of the blood that was shed," it instantly becomes as white as snow on Alpine peaks; pure as the waters of mid-ocean, which the stain of the great city cannot soil; transparent as the blue ether which is the curtain of the tabernacle of the Most High.[1]

For Further Study
1. Write your own psalm of repentance to the Lord as David did, expressing to Him the desires of your heart.
2. Do a word study of *heart*, following the directions in chapter 1.
3. Familiarize yourself with the content of Psalm 51 and ask a friend to quiz you on it.

•TOOL CHEST•
(A Suggested Optional Resource)

CHARACTER STUDY BOOKS
Character studies paint life sketches of Bible characters by tracing their backgrounds and development through the pages of Scripture. This particular type of book seeks to provide its reader with lessons learned from the lives and faith of biblical personalities. They are more than historical documentaries or straightforward biographies in that they ask penetrating questions of the figure under study and attempt to find answers from the biblical data. Character studies are inspiring and challenging literature with which to line your library shelves. Here are just a few title ideas of good character studies on the life of David.

> *The King and the Kingdom* by William Barclay (Baker Books, 1980)
> *Ordinary Men Called by God* by James Montgomery Boice (Victor Books, 1982)
> *A Heart for God* by Stuart Briscoe (Thomas Nelson, 1984)
> *David: A Man after the Heart of God* (Back to the Bible, 1985)
> *David* by F.B. Meyer (Christian Literature Crusade, 1977)

4

Taming Our Tongues

•FOOD FOR THOUGHT•

A Christian is a mind through which Christ thinks, a heart through which Christ loves, and a voice through which Christ speaks. The instrument of the voice is the tongue, which "pure religion" (James 1:27) should affect.

Solomon has aptly said, "A wise man holds his tongue. Only a fool blurts out everything he knows; that only leads to sorrow and trouble" (Prov. 10:14). I'm sure all of us have suffered from "foot-in-mouth" disease at least once in our lifetime. How well I remember being totally humiliated after remarking to a young student at Bible school that I had heard that the visiting speaker for the week was very boring. "I am?" a voice at my side inquired. It was the guest speaker whom I had never met, and who had quietly joined the group of people I was talking to. Oh, how I wished in that awful moment that I had heeded Solomon's warning: "Don't talk so much. You keep putting your foot in your mouth. Be sensible and turn off the flow!" (Prov. 10:19)

One of the best ways to remind ourselves how much trouble our tongues can cause is use an acrostic, which is what I've done here.

T stands for *trouble.* The tongue is a small part of the body, yet has such great potential for causing trouble (James 3:5). James used two graphic pictures to illustrate the power of the tongue: the rudder of a ship and the bit in a horse's mouth (James 3:3-5). Jesus Christ can help us rudder our speech and reign-in our runaway tongues. He, Himself, was the perfect model of such restraint. The very night He was betrayed—knowing that He had only a very short time left with His disciples—He said, "I have much more to say to you, more than you can now bear" (John 16:12). What restraint! I'm sure if I had been in His position, I would have bent the disciples' ears all night.

T also stands for *truth*—truth that can harness any trouble the

46

tongue can cause. It takes so few words to steer a wayward conversation back on track. Not long ago, I was having lunch with some ladies and one of them said, "I hear Mrs. Riley was voted in as president of the church women." No problem with that. The ship was sailing along in the most pleasant and placid of waters. But then the little rudder gently steered the vessel toward a whirlpool. "And I don't know what I think about that," the lady imparting the information continued, "particularly since I have heard she is having trouble in her marriage."

The neat thing about the tongue, of course, is that the little rudder that can so easily turn a conversation off course, can also steer the conversation back on course again. "Oh, I don't know where you heard that," I said. "I certainly have heard no such thing, and I think she is an excellent choice!" Now some of you may object, thinking perhaps that the lady was right and I should have set up a Watergate tribunal on the spot. Maybe, but I believe, as Spurgeon did, that "a lie travels around the world while truth is putting on her boots." I hoped that I had at least given truth a headstart.

James' commentary on the tongue apparently came about because some people in the church wanted the prestige of being teachers. Human ambition had driven them to the point of demanding teaching positions, without their necessarily having the natural ability, spiritual gift, or doctrinal knowledge to do so. James deals succinctly with this problem, commenting that teachers will be judged all the more severely, and therefore, people shouldn't seek to teach. At this point in the passage, James changes his focus and begins talking about obscenity (James 3:9-12).

O stands for *obscenity*, part of which is profanity. "With the tongue . . . we curse men, who have been made in God's likeness," James says (3:9). Exodus 20:7 says, "You shall not misuse the name of the Lord your God, for the Lord will not hold anyone guiltless who misuses His name." The last part of this verse alone should be enough to make us bridle our tongues—for "the Lord will not hold him guiltless who takes His name in vain." But what exactly does that phrase mean? It means that God looks on that man as a criminal and will severely punish him. We must not speak lightly or irreverently of the Lord. It also means that idle words shall be judged. The casual "Oh God" or "Oh Christ" or deviations of His holy name like "golly" and "gosh," will be treated with equal severity. We need to make sure that our children understand how serious this sort of language is.

Not only is profanity out, but cursing is too (James 3:9). Since we have been made in God's image, cursing man is like cursing God. "Out of the same mouth comes praise and cursings," says James. "My brothers, this should not be" (James 3:10). It's useless to go to church on Sunday and sing the hymns, then use angry, abusive words of those we consider our subordinates in their absence. "Can both fresh water and salt water flow from the same spring?" the brother of our Lord inquired (James 3:11).

N is for *nagging*. "Turning off the flow" is a tricky business for the nag. The nag always needs a bridle in the mouth. Solomon, perhaps from bitter experience, exclaims, "A quarrelsome wife is like a constant dripping on a rainy day" (Prov. 27:15). And why is it we nag? Perhaps because we have not forgiven. Nagging, after all, could be defined as unforgiveness showing. For example, have you ever heard a wife say to her husband, "Are you going to forget my birthday again like you did last year?" It's obvious that this wife has neither forgotten nor forgiven her husband!

G represents *gossip*, which is the needless repetition of real or imagined faults. "Likewise the tongue is a small part of the body, but it makes great boasts. Consider what a great forest is set on fire by a small spark. The tongue also is a fire, a world of evil among the parts of the body. It corrupts the whole person, sets the whole course of his life on fire, and is itself set on fire by hell" (James 3:5-6). What do we do with a forest fire? If we are on the spot, we can decide not to add fuel to the flames. "Fire goes out for lack of fuel, and tensions disappear when gossip stops" (Prov. 26:20). Knowing it only takes a spark to get a fire going, I can put my "log" down and keep any tidbits of personal information I know about another person well away from the consuming flames of gossip. Doing this will stop the "hot" news right there. James, who understood the diabolical nature of the human tongue, wrote that it "keeps the wheel of our existence red hot!" In other words, "the tongue can make the whole of life a blazing hell!"

Have you ever heard someone say, "Don't let this go any further; it needs to be kept confidential," then seen that person pass on the information to the very next person he/she met? Scripture says, "A gossip betrays a confidence, but a trustworthy man keeps a secret" (Prov. 11:13). Why couldn't we all decide to find something nice to say or not to say anything at all?

U stands for *untruth* or the half-lie. Exaggeration, perhaps, is a part of this. I love to tell a good story. But I have to watch when I'm speaking that I do not let my tongue run away with me as I'm tempted to speak "evang*elastic*ally." When listening to statements other people are making that we suspect are lies, we can always say something like, "Let's find the facts and get them straight," or "Let's ask an uninvolved person to give us an opinion."

E stands for *envy*, which springs from a grudging contemplation of one more fortunate than oneself. Such "sour grapes" does not befit the "branch" created to bear the fruit of the Spirit.

S stands for *slander*. Its sting is like that of a snake bite—quick and often deadly. The problem is, many times there is a particle of truth in what is being said. Slander colors the facts, leaving out one detail and adding another. It is as if two men had painted pictures of the same object—one having painted the object in perspective, while the other has the object filling the page.

The love of finding fault must be given up. Jesus alone is Judge—and that of the living and the dead (Acts 10:42). All too often we presume to tell Him, "You judge the dead and I'll look after the living for You!" Seeing as how the devil is the accuser of the brethren, we must be careful not to be found doing his work for him. It was Socrates who said, "Speak that I may *see* thee." Wouldn't you have thought he would have said, "Speak that I may *hear* thee"? But no! I think Socrates would have thoroughly appreciated James 3:1-12.

It is as a person speaks that we get a glimpse of the real person who lives inside the body. The tongue tells more than the information of the moment; it reveals one's character, attitude, and philosophy of life. Perhaps we need to listen to ourselves for a little while. We may hear things we don't like very much—things that will make us sorry or ashamed. Then we can put our tongues to good use—confessing our sins, praising our God, and sharing the good news that God will give us the power to control one of the smallest, but surely most unruly of all our body members—the tongue.

•TALKING IT OVER•

1. REVIEW AND MEMORIZE.   *10 minutes*
   Review James 3:1-12 and answer the following
   questions:
   ☐ Which problem of the tongue do you struggle
   with the most? (Circle one.)

   Truth   Obscenity   Nagging   Gossip

   Unruliness   Envy   Slander

   ☐ Circle the illustration which most helped you
   understand how much trouble your tongue can
   cause. Discuss.

   Rudder and ship   Bitter and sweet water

   Forest and fire   Branches and fruit

   Snake bite   Bit and horse

   ☐ Pick one verse from James 3:1-12 and spend a
   few minutes now memorizing it.

2. READ AND DISCUSS.   *10 minutes*
   The devil is called the "accuser of the brethren,"
   therefore, we must be careful not to do his work
   for him.
   ☐ Read Genesis 3:1-4. What do you learn about
   Satan's tongue from this passage?
   ☐ Reread the passage, this time observing Eve.
   What do you learn about her tongue?
   ☐ What is one valuable lesson in this passage you
   need to apply to your own life?

3. RELATE AND SHARE.   *10 minutes*
   Have you ever been the victim of someone else's
   judging tongue? Look at 1 Corinthians 4:1-16 to
   see what Paul said about judging other people.
   What lessons do you learn from this passage?

•PRAYING IT THROUGH•

Suggested Times

---

1. (As a group) Use your tongues to: *5 minutes*
   □ Praise God.
   □ Bless men.
   □ Intercede for those whose tongues criticize and
   persecute you.

---

2. (Silently, on your own) Pray about: *3 minutes*
   □ A specific problem with your own tongue the
   Lord has convicted you of today.
   □ The verse from James 3:1-12 you memorized.

---

3. Choose a prayer partner and . . .   *10 minutes*
   □ Pray for those whose tongues tell you there is
   something wrong with their hearts.
   □ Share one way you would like to use your
   tongue for *good* this week.

---

4. Finish your time of prayer by praying together the   *2 minutes*
   Lord's Prayer.

   Our Father who art in heaven, hallowed be Thy name.
   Thy kingdom come. Thy will be done in earth,
   As it is in heaven.
   Give us this day our daily bread.
   And forgive us our debts, as we forgive our debtors.
   And lead us not into temptation,
   But deliver us from evil:
   For Thine is the kingdom, and the power,
   And the glory, forever. Amen.

•DIGGING DEEPER•

James 3:1-12

1. Read through James 3:1-12 twice, taking time to write down all the things you observe in the passage that are significant. Your observations should summarize the main ideas and content of the passage without simply rewriting the verses. Always keep in mind that when observing a passage you are attempting to answer the question, "What do I see?" Try to come up with a list of fifteen or twenty observations from James 3:1-12.

1. _____

2. _____

3. _____

4. _____

5. _____

6. _____

7. _____

8. _____

9. _____

10. _____

11. _____

12. _____

13. _____

14. _____

15. _____

16. _____

17. _____

18. _____

19. _____

20. _____

2. Now, imagine yourself to be a journalist, or better yet, a detective, and study James 3:1-12 again, this time asking such key questions as: Who? What? Where? When? and Why? For example, you might ask these questions of the text you are studying: Who is addressing whom? What is the main topic of discussion? What are the recurring words, phrases, or ideas? Where is the action taking place? Where was the author when he wrote the book and where were the recipients when they received it? When were these words penned? Save the *Why?* question for last, working on answering questions of this type only after you have answered as many of the other questions as you can. You may wish to list your answers to these key questions in categories to help you think more clearly.

Who?

What?

Where?

When?

Why?

3. Look for the following structural elements in James 3:1-12. (Identifying the principles of structure will help you see how the author organized his thoughts in the passage.) NOTE: If you are completing this Bible study as a group, have each member look for one element and report their findings to the group.

COMPARISON: the association of like things.
CONTRAST: the association of things which are opposite.
REPETITION: the reiteration of the same or similar terms, phrases, clauses, or concepts.
CAUSE TO EFFECT: the statement of a cause and then its effects.
EFFECT TO CAUSE: the opposite of cause to effect; the statement or description of the effect(s) and then their cause(s).

EXPLANATION: the introduction of an idea which is then expanded or explained.

ILLUSTRATION: the introduction of an idea, followed by an illustration (example) of it.

CLIMAX: the arrangement of the text in such a way that it progresses from the lesser to the greater (i.e., the story or discourse builds to a climax).

PIVOT: the arrangement of subject matter so that there are pivotal points at which the story changes direction; they act like hinges in the text.

INTERCHANGE: the alteration or exchange of certain elements in the text; movement of the author back and forth between several ideas.

PREPARATION: the inclusion of background material or the setting for events or ideas to prepare the reader to understand that which follows.

SUMMARY: the gathering together of main ideas by the author in order to clarify his thoughts; he seeks to express and then restate them in summary form.

QUESTION POSED: the structuring of the text around questions which the author raises.

QUESTION ANSWERED: the structuring of the text around answers the author gives to a question, be it explicitly stated or merely implied.[1]

What did you find?

4. Keeping all that you have observed in mind, reread James 3:1-12 and identify the main idea of each paragraph in a concise, single sentence.

Paragraph   Verses   Main Idea

1   1-2

2

3

4

5. What is the major point of verses 3-12?

6. Why do you think James needed to address this issue with the church of his day?

7. Do you ever struggle with the problems Paul's readers had?

8. Look over all of James 3. What solutions for your struggles do you find in this chapter?

9. Identify one way in which your tongue frequently speaks in an unwise manner. Pray for "wisdom from heaven" to help you tame your tongue. Then ask two friends to regularly pray for you and let them know each week how you are progressing.

For Further Study
1. Read two commentaries on James 3:1-12 to see how closely your observations match those of the commentators. What do they identify as the central theme of the passage? What reasons do they give for James addressing this subject?

•TOOL CHEST•
(A Suggested Optional Resource)

UNLOCKING THE SCRIPTURES
The study tool used in this lesson's Digging Deeper section was *Unlocking the Scriptures* by Hans Finzel (Victor Books, 1986). Exciting principles and methods of inductive Bible study are contained in this 144-page book, which both the novice and experienced Bible student will find helpful. A handy paperback, *Unlocking the Scriptures* detailedly defines and walks the reader through the inductive process of observation, interpretation, and application. With the help of this useful study tool, one can learn how to study a passage within its context, discover the theme of a Bible book, and accurately apply Bible truths to everyday life.

Many good inductive Bible study guides are on the market today and come in convenient paperback editions. Generally, their cost is under $10. Besides *Unlocking the Scriptures*, other titles to choose from in this book category include:

Opening the Book by Hans Finzel (Victor Books, 1987)
A Layman's Guide to Studying the Bible by Walter Henrichsen (Zondervan, 1985)
Asking Questions by D. Bruce Lockerbie (Matt Media, 1980)
The Joy of Discovery in Bible Study by Oletta Wald (Augsburg, 1975)
12 Dynamic Bible Study Methods (Victor Books, 1981)

5
Helping Hands

•FOOD FOR THOUGHT•

Have you ever noticed that hands have their own body language? We wring our hands with anxiety, fiddle with our fingers when we are bored, or shake our fists in someone's face when we are angry. Hands can be social too—greeting friends, waving hello, or hugging those we love. Often it is in the helping skills that our hands speak most eloquently to those around us.

What our hands do tells our world a lot about who we are and whom we serve. We can use our hands to care for our own needs, or we can use them to help those in trouble as we see in the life of the woman of Proverbs 31 who "extended her hands to the needy" (Prov. 31:20).

Sometimes, however, we do good things with our hands that confuse those who are watching us, leading them to believe that we are trying to earn brownie points with God. At times, good hands doing good works need to be explained with good words so that nobody gets the wrong idea. I have talked to people who really believe that if they *do* good things, they will get to heaven. In fact, a survey was taken in our local area not long ago that asked the question, "Do you believe you will go to heaven when you die?" Eighty-three percent of the people answering the poll said, "Yes." When asked, "On what grounds?" the majority of the respondents replied, "Based on the way I've lived my life up to this moment." Now that's a rather scary thing, because it means that an awful lot of people are very sincere. Unfortunately, they are sincerely wrong! If we were talking about going to Florida or some other state, it wouldn't really matter. But we're not—we are talking about going to heaven, and the Bible clearly states that we won't get to heaven through our own efforts. We are not saved by our own hand; it is the hand of God that saves us.

How is it we are saved? First of all, we are saved by *grace*. God's grace gives us what we do not deserve. And what don't we deserve? Heaven! We do not deserve heaven because we are sinners and sinners deserve hell. Second, it is through *faith* that we are saved. That means faith in *Him* and what *He* has done to get us to heaven, not what we have done to get ourselves there!

So, what, if anything, should our hands do? They should be clasped in prayer as we cast ourselves at His feet and plead for His mercy, asking Him to forgive our sins and enter our lives by His Spirit. Then, when that is settled, our hands should begin to work for Him. Not in order to earn eternal merit, but in simple gratitude for what He has earned for us. Christians are not saved *by* their works, they are saved *to do* good works. In other words, we are not to "serve to be saved," but rather are to "be saved to serve." Ephesians 2:10 tells us we are His "workmanship, created in Christ Jesus to do good works."

Our works should grow out of our worship. It is at His feet that we get a correct idea of the value of work. And it is at His feet that we receive instructions concerning our hands! Paul came to the conclusion that he should "labor, struggling with all His energy, which so powerfully works in me" (Col. 1:29). Paul's idea about work, I'm certain, came out of his worship experience.

Once I needed to raise money to build a youth center for teenagers. As I worshiped at Jesus' feet, He gave me the most practical idea: "I can begin with a nursery school," I thought, "which will generate income to pay the youth workers and at the same time provide Christian day care for the community." My heart inspired by the Holy Spirit, and my mind stimulated by the Word of God, resulted in my hands getting to work! And I learned a valuable lesson: I cannot expect other people to put their hands to work until I've first exercised my own.

Getting a nursery school started takes a lot of money, which is something we had very little of. But what we lacked in money, we made up for in resourcefulness! We made building blocks for the children with the ends of planks we begged off a local builder down the road. Sanding and varnishing these would-be toys took five or six of us weeks, but at last our magnificent barrel full of blocks was ready for the little ones who would use them to build anything from dog houses to small towns. Scrubbing, painting, varnishing, and sewing followed. My hands became rough and raw, and my fingernails broken with all the hard work. I'm afraid they were not very beautiful to look at. But then, they say "beauty is in the eye of the beholder," and I knew, without a shadow of a doubt, that when I got to heaven the Beholder would take my hands in His, turn them over, and smile at me. In the end, that was all that mattered!

Our wonder-working God also knows the wisdom of work! Work gives us a sense of usefulness and worth because it can have eternal value. For this reason, we feel a sense of fulfillment when we do what is necessary for our families, the church, or the world. When Jesus saw a man with a withered hand, he healed him! (Mark 3:1-5) I'm sure He knew that one of the most humiliating things that can ever happen to a man is to be out of work and unable to use his hands to provide for the physical needs of his family. God understands how we human beings think—"If what I *do* matters, then *I* matter."

I've always found joy in working for Jesus! Even though Stuart and I have arrived at the "empty nest" time of life, we have found no time to sit idly by, twiddling our thumbs. After all, our "nest" needs to be kept ready for all the birds in the world with broken wings whom God may send our way! Each of us needs to look for a need and meet it. This will most certainly entail practical work, but it will also bring certain satisfaction!

Believing that work is ordained of God can transform our "Nazareth living." Daily doings will become important and significant. I have a friend who has a plaque hanging over her kitchen sink which reads, "Divine service conducted here three times daily." I like that. To wash the dishes as if Jesus were going to eat from them, to clean the shoes as if He were going to wear them, to make the beds ready in the guest room as if He were to take His rest there elevates housework to an altogether new plane. If we will learn to do it all "as unto the Lord" (Col. 3:23), then we will find each day filled with special meaning. What's more, when others see not only our good works but also our good attitudes about them, they will glorify our Taskmaster!

Works can, however, take their toll. The very word *work* tells us there is effort involved. Works are work! Energy will need to be expended, sacrifices will have to be made, someone will have to pay the price. I can't help but think of those load-laden donkeys in the Old Testament that were used to do the "donkey work"! Like them, someone has to do the dirty work. Why not me? The sad part is, there are too many people in churches today who are only too happy to put the load on the donkey rather than carry it themselves.

I remember asking myself, "Why not me?" as I scrubbed the filthy floors in the old grain warehouse we were turning into a nursery school. I was tempted to tell one of the teens to pick up the dead cat

I had just discovered in the corner of the cellar and get rid of it. But why should their hands do the dirty work when mine were available? In those busy days I learned many hard lessons about hard work, not least of which was "Whatever you do, work at it with all your heart" (Col. 3:23). Commitment is a major part of it. Jesus, praying to His Father, said, "I have brought you glory on earth by completing the work You gave me to do" (John 17:4). He did not say, "I have half-finished the work," or "I've barely finished it!" No, Jesus fully finished the work God had given Him to do! How many times I start things and never finish them. May God find us faithful in *finishing* the "good works" He has ordained beforehand that we should do.

The Bible tells us that "He has prepared" the works that are waiting for us. "But how do I know what they are?" you ask. You will know by staying in touch with the Lord and doing the next obvious thing. Start by stretching out your hands to the needy where you live—in your city, or town, or even in your own neighborhood. If you will take the first step, you will most certainly know what comes next!

Knowing what to do with our hands is very much an individual thing. In fact, only we can discover it for ourselves—no one else can tell us what works our hands are to do. And we can discover our hands' work by first giving them to God in a definite act of personal consecration, followed by daily requests for divine direction. Because these marvelous instruments of the body are so capable and dexterous, we will have to determine which of a multitude of possible options are ours for the doing. These doings may differ daily. One day, God may instruct us to use our hands to care for the tasks at home, while someone else's hands are put to good use at a typewriter or pushing a pen. Another day, our fingers may need to hold a book or study materials. Or they may be used to relax the whole body by picking up a tennis racquet or basketball. Other times our hands may be found tending the sick or carrying food to the bereaved. How wonderfully designed are these instruments of good works. May He who said, "Occupy till I come" (Luke 19:13) find us busy doing His will with our hands until He comes to take us home!

•TALKING IT OVER•

---

1. DISCUSS TOGETHER.

    ☐ How would you explain to a "good" person that he/she is not *good enough* for God? (Try to think of Scriptures to back up your answer.)

    ☐ Have you ever thought of housework as being ordained of God? How might this thought help you transform your daily duties into works of worship?

    ☐ What aspect of your "Nazareth living" will be affected by today's lesson?

10 minutes

---

2. EVALUATE PERSONALLY.

    ☐ What sort of *works* are hard for you to do? Why are they hard?

    ☐ What are the costs involved? The commitment required? The consequences in doing works of this kind?

    ☐ Reread Ephesians 2:8-10 again. Which phrase in these verses offers you a sense of assurance in doing the hard "works" of faith you listed in the previous question?

10 minutes

---

3. READ AND APPLY.
Read Matthew 25:31-46. This passage describes some of the works God is waiting for us to do. Where should we begin? With the thing closest at hand!

    ☐ What is that one thing in Matthew 25:31-46 you will do? When will you get started?

    ☐ Talk about it with a friend in the group.

    ☐ Pray about it together.

10 minutes

•PRAYING IT THROUGH•

Suggested Times

---

1. (Corporately) Praise God for:
   □ Creating for us things we enjoy doing with our hands.
   □ His redemptive work on our behalf and His provision of the Holy Spirit who helps us do His will.
   □ The good works He has prepared for us to do.

5 minutes

---

2. (Corporately) Pray for:
   □ People you know (first name only) who are under the false impression that good works will save them.
   □ People who have been saved by grace, but for one reason or another are not producing good works in their lives.
   □ People in God's work who are overworked because the underworked people do not understand this truth.
   □ Specific things that need to be done in your fellowship that are not getting done because no one will do them.

10 minutes

---

3. (In twos) Share with each other one good work you believe God has given you to do. What is hard about this work? Pray for each other in this regard.

5 minutes

•DIGGING DEEPER•

Ephesians 2:1-10

OBSERVATION

1. *Contrast,* according to *The American Heritage Dictionary,* is defined as "to set in opposition in order to show or emphasize differences" and "to show differences when compared." Slowly read through Ephesians 2:1-10. These ten verses are filled with contrasts. Make a list of all the contrasts you see.

2. What is God's diagnosis of human nature? (v. 3)

3. How is our relationship to God described in verse 3?

   In verse 4?

4. Look up the word *grace* in a dictionary. How is it defined?

5. Note the words in Ephesians 2:1-10 that are repeated. Which words are repeated for emphasis?

6. According to verse 10, why were we created?

INTERPRETATION
7. What does it mean to be "dead in your transgressions and sins"? (v. 5)

Check your answer against the following excerpts from two secondary sources: Vine's *An Expository Dictionary of New Testament Words* and Wuest's *Word Studies in the Greek New Testament.*

DEAD
A. Noun and Adjective

NEKROS (νεκρόω) is used of *(a)* the death of the body, cp. Jas. 2:26, its most frequent sense: *(b)* the actual spiritual condition of unsaved men, Matt. 8:22; John 5:25; Eph. 2:1, 5; 5:14; Phil. 3:11; Col. 2:13; cp. Luke 15:24: *(c)* the ideal spiritual condition of believers in regard to sin, Rom. 6:11: *(d)* a church in declension, inasmuch as in that state it is inactive and barren, Rev. 3:1: *(e)* sin, which apart from law cannot produce a sense of guilt, Rom. 7:8: *(f)* the body of the believer in contrast to his spirit, Rom. 8:10: *(g)* the works of the Law, inasmuch as, however good in themselves, Rom. 7:13, they cannot produce life, Heb. 6:1; 9:14: *(h)* the faith that does not produce works, Jas. 2:17, 26; cp. ver. 20.[1]

The word "dead" is *nekros*, "spiritually dead, that is, destitute of a life that recognizes and is devoted to God, because given up to trespasses and sins, inactive as respects doing right." It should be kept clearly in mind that death is not extinction of being or inactivity. Spiritual death is the state of separation from God and His life. Death itself is a separation, whether physical, the separation of the person from his body, or spiritual, the separation of the person from God.
The state of death spoken of here is "in trespasses and sins." It is the dative of reference, "dead with reference to

trespasses and sins." That is, this state of death had to do with trespasses and sins. It was not physical death, although that is caused in the last analysis by sin. This state of death was linked with trespasses and sins in that it had to do with the moral and ethical part of the individual, his reason, will, and emotions. He was living in a state of separation from God and His life in that the latter did not energize and control the reason, will, and emotions of the person. These were very active, but were energized by the totally depraved nature. The word "trespasses" is the translation of *paraptōma* from *parapiptō*, "to fall beside a person or thing, to slip aside, hence, to deviate from the right path, to turn aside, to wander." Thus, in the word *paraptōma*, sin is looked upon as a lapse or deviation from truth or uprightness, a trespass, a misdeed. "Sins" is the rendering of *hamartia* from *hamartanō*, "to miss the mark." It was used in the Greek classics of a spearman missing the target at which he aimed the spear. It was used in the ethical terminology of the Greeks to mean "to fail of one's purpose, to go wrong." In the N.T., it speaks of sin as the act of a person failing to obey the Word of God, failing to measure up in his life to the will of God. Its use is excellently illustrated in Romans 3:23, "All have sinned (missed the mark), and at present come short of the glory of God." The mark or target is the glory of God. Man was created to glorify God. His attempt, where the attempt is made, to live a life pleasing to God, falls short of the target, like a spear thrown by an athlete, falls short of the target at which it is thrown.[2]

8. How can we reconcile being "objects of [God's] wrath" with the idea of God's "great love for us"? (v. 4)

9. What do the following Scripture passages add to your understanding of what it means to be "alive in Christ"?

Romans 6:1-10

Ephesians 4:17–5:2

Colossians 3:1-10

10. Explain what verse 6 of Ephesians 2 means.

11. What has God's grace—mentioned in verse 8—saved us from?

12. Ephesians 2:8-9 makes it clear that we could never do anything to earn God's acceptance or to get Him to like us. His acceptance of us is based entirely on our putting our faith in His Son, our Lord Jesus Christ. What are some ways you have tried to earn God's acceptance and/or approval?

REFLECTION
13. Recall a time when someone completely surprised you and gave you a gift you did not deserve. How did you feel?

14. Reflect on these four phrases from Romans 6.

☐ *"Shall we go on sinning?"* (6:1) Which response should the undeserved favor of God in our lives prompt: A desire to continue in sin? Or an attitude of gratefulness which wants to leave behind and run away as far as possible from a life of sin?

☐ *"We too may live a new life"* (6:4). What are the characteristics of a new life in Christ? Do they accurately describe my life?

67

☐ *"We should no longer be slaves to sin"* (6:6). We are no longer enslaved by the powerful hold of sin in our lives as we were before we became Christians. Christ's power has set us free and enables us to live moral and obedient lives.

☐ *"Offer the parts of your body to Him as instruments of righteousness"* (6:13). How can God use my hands as instruments of righteousness?

APPLICATION

15. Paul describes God's act of grace toward us in Christ Jesus as an expression of His "kindness to us." In what other ways has God expressed His kindness to you?

16. What good works has God prepared for you to do?

If you are unsure, then ask yourself, "What unmet needs exist . . .

among the members of my Bible study?

in my church?

in my neighborhood?

in my community?

17. Ask God to show you where He wants you "to do good works." If you are wondering where to begin, find something that needs doing, put your hands to it, and begin. In prayer, continue asking God to confirm His direction to you in the doing of it.

For Further Study

1. Memorize Ephesians 2:8-9.
2. Research the meaning of the phrase "in the coming ages" (v. 7).

•TOOL CHEST•
(A Suggested Optional Resource)

WORD STUDY HELPS

Word study helps enhance the English reader's understanding of Greek and Hebrew word usages. When you come to a difficult word or phrase in Scripture, turn to a study aid of this type to learn the origin and historical development of the word in question. This sort of study tool functions much like an English language dictionary in this regard: some are listed in alphabetical order. Others are listed by Bible book, chapter, and verse. The two word study helps which appeared in the Digging Deeper section of this lesson were:

> *An Expository Dictionary of New Testament Words* by W.E. Vine (Revell)
> *Word Studies in the Greek New Testament* by Kenneth S. Wuest (Eerdmans)

6

Fitting Our Feet

•FOOD FOR THOUGHT•

(GROUP LEADER, NOTE: *You may want to read the following testimony aloud.*)

Metaphorically speaking, feet talk of the Christian walk. Scripture tells us we should walk after the Spirit (Rom. 8:1, 4)—in newness of life (Rom. 6:4) and in wisdom (Col. 4:5) and truth (3 John 4). But our physical feet tell a tale as well. They tell us where in this wild world of ours we've been. If only we would recognize the importance of our footprints! Imagine having dye on the soles of your feet so that everyone could see where and what you'd been up to all your life. Would you want to rub out some of the tracks? Have you ever noticed the maps at the back of your Bible with the footprints of Jesus and the Apostle Paul laid out on the pages? Would you . . . would I want my life—like theirs—to be etched on the pages of a book for all the world to see? As I thought about this, I began to retrace my own footprints in the sands of time.

In my mind's eye, I saw my footprints as a toddler in Liverpool, England, running to the dugout bomb shelter my father had made for our family. It was wartime. And my family and I lived in an area of the country where there were dockyards which enemy war planes bombed night after night. Even though I was pretty small at the time, I had some big questions, such as, "If God lives in heaven, why doesn't He stop the airplanes from dropping death from the sky?"

One night a bomb was dropped too close for comfort and the footprints of our family changed direction as we ran away to the comparative safety of the beautiful English Lake District. This is where we stayed until after the war was over. Then our footprints headed off once more to Liverpool.

It was about this time—as I came into my teenage years—that my feet began to travel down some pretty perverse paths. Chasing after affirmation, I donned skating boots, tennis shoes, and dancing slippers—my body language shouting all the while, "Hey, look at me! I need to be center stage in your thinking." I communicated my need for affirmation by stamping my feet, trampling over anyone who got in my way, and covering up my tracks afterward! Had I been in the habit of reading the Bible at the time, I may well have come across Proverbs 6:28, which states, "Can a man walk on hot coals without his feet being scorched?" Perhaps reading such a salutary warning would have changed the direction my life was taking.

Next, my 18-year-old feet donned high heel shoes and trotted off to a teacher training college in Cambridge where I began to tread a profound path, walking down academic trails that at first seemed fascinating, but which in the end led nowhere. Then on to the hospital. With feet tucked securely in bed, I remember the fear I felt as I waited for the doctors to diagnose my mysterious ailment. Standing in my little fuzzy bedroom slippers in an antiseptic hospital ward, I listened as the girl in the next bed told an incredible story about a pair of feet in another day and age that had been nailed to a cross for my sake. And for the first time in my life, I found myself standing on holy ground!

Have *you* ever stood on holy ground? Have you met God as you've wandered through the labyrinth of life and had Him turn you around and tell you to follow Him? Taking off my soiled footwear (you always have to do this when you stand on holy ground), I donned my Gospel shoes and was headed heavenward. I seem to remember Jesus, my newfound Saviour, saying as we set off together, "Follow Me. Stay close by My side" . . . and I knew He knew the way I would take.

I found the Lord Jesus to be such a gentle friend. Quite content to let me take small steps at first, He ever encouraged me to keep in step with His Spirit. I learned early on, through sorrow and sometimes confusion, that when I was in step with God, I was often out of step with others, even some of my closest friends who at the time were not in step with Him. One time, for instance, I received an invitation to go to a risqué party. Opening my guidebook, the Bible, I found this piece of sage advice: "Keep your foot from evil" (Prov. 4:27). "Well—that's pretty straightforward!" I thought. What I learned is that I must not walk straightaway into temptation and expect God to deliver me from evil. Rather, I am "to walk worthy of the vocation wherewith [I am] called" (Eph. 4:1). Sometimes this meant literally walking away from things that occupied my time and attention. It was at this particular point that I hung up my dancing slippers until I could trust myself to wear them again. But because my feet were dancing to a different tune, I didn't miss the dance floor one little bit!

My footprints then turned back toward Liverpool, taking me to a group of rough, tough kids in the city school system who needed someone to tell them the good news about a new way of life. One here and one there began telling me, "How beautiful on the mountains are the feet of those who bring good news" (Isa. 52:7), and I found this to be a thrilling ministry that took me to the wildest places.

God's Word reminded me that I was to go to the lost—to those who had never heard the Good News. And I was to go where the lost were, even if it meant climbing mountains to reach them. I suppose one might say that "mountains" are the most difficult places to go. I learned to go with the Word of God, telling forth plainly the Good News, for "how can they hear without someone preaching to them?" (Rom. 10:14) My feet followed the Shepherd into coffee bars and youth haunts to kids who were looking for life and finding only trouble.

All of this eventually led my footsteps toward another pair of feet— to those of a British banker, Stuart Briscoe! Bridal steps followed in good time, and we discovered the joy of two pairs of feet walking along the same path together. After a few years, three other little pairs of footprints joined ours—David's, Judy's, and Peter's. For a while my mother-feet chased childish feet from playground, to school, to house, bath, and bed. We shared our waking hours together, discovering the joy of family and enriching the lives of all whose feet crowded together under our kitchen table. Those were days when father's footsteps traveled the world alone, ministering to needy people while we traipsed daily to the letter box for news.

Looking back at my map of life's footprints, I can see that I've traveled down some pretty rough roads, as well as on more pleasant paths of peace. There have been slippery places along the way, wet with tears of loneliness and defeat, but with each footstep I've seen that "He has preserved [my] life and kept [my] feet from slipping" (Ps. 66:9). When I remember my stumbling steps and see the gaping holes dug by the devil to trip me up, I see clearly that Jesus has gone before me, making "the crooked places straight" (Isa. 45:2), and I am glad.

Above all, I can see in retrospect that He had indeed given me "hinds' feet" for those high places (Ps. 18:33). The highest places have often been the lowest points in my life, and yet, He has provided exactly the right footwear to carry me through. Whether I've needed a pair of spiritual high heels to step beyond myself into ministry with the "up and outers," donned a pair of boots for a missions trip, or slipped on my Reeboks for some wild campus challenge, He has always equipped me with just the right footwear to do the job. And what is my part? Simply to put on the appropriate footwear He's provided and follow Him. One thing is certain—there are to be no slippers for me yet! Slippers are for heavenly home and fireside. They are for the "then," not the "now"!

Tell me, friend—as you trace *your* footprints in the sands of time, where have you been? Where do your feet stand now? Where are they headed? The starting place for each one of us is that holy piece of ground at the foot of the Cross. I would love to help any of you who are reading this to "take off your shoes"—to see God as He is, waiting to receive you, and holy, even though you are not. If you have never stood before Him to ask Him to be your Saviour, you can do so now. Make my words your own, if you like, and pray:

> Lord Jesus, I believe You walked this earth as God in human form. I understand that Your feet were pierced on the cross for my sake and that You suffered and died for me. I believe You took my place and punishment so that I might walk free. Thank You, Jesus! I now invite Your Spirit to enter my life so that I may have the power to follow You wherever You lead me. Here I stand, on holy ground. Save me, Lord, I pray in Jesus' name. Amen.

If you in all sincerity have made this prayer your own, tell your group leader, a friend, or your pastor about it. Then make sure your footprints head off from this experience in the right direction— behind His!

•TALKING IT OVER•

---

1. REFLECT AND SHARE.

   9 minutes

   ☐ (Individually) Take a few minutes to think about the "footprints" of your life.

   ☐ (In twos) Identify *one* of the most important crossroads of your life or something Jesus has helped you face when you've felt like running away from it.

---

2. READ AND DISCUSS.

   7 minutes

   Read Exodus 3:1-6. Then discuss the following questions as a group.

   ☐ Moses was standing on holy ground when God called him to follow. *Where* do you have to be for God to appear to you in a special way?

   ☐ What sort of things can we do to cultivate a sense of awe when God speaks to us?

---

3. READ AND REFLECT.

   7 minutes

   ☐ Which path/road are you traveling at this time?

A pleasant path	A rough road
A perverse path	A high road
A profound path	The road home

   ☐ Read Psalm 23. Which verse appeals to your particular and immediate situation? Why?

---

4. STUDY WITH A PARTNER.

   7 minutes

   Look up the following verses to see what Scripture teaches us about our spiritual walk. Share your findings as a group.

Romans 3:10-12	Ephesians 2:8-10
Romans 6:4	Colossians 2:13-15
Romans 8:4	Colossians 4:5-6
Romans 13:13-14	2 Thessalonians 2:7
2 Corinthians 5:7	2 John 4

•PRAYING IT THROUGH•

Suggested Times

1. (Quietly reflect) Have you ever stood on holy ground? The holiest ground of all is at the foot of the Cross. Close your eyes and thank Jesus right now for dying for you. Then ask Him to help you to follow Him closely, and praise Him for providing for you the right footwear—your Gospel shoes.

5 minutes

2. (Corporately) Pray for:
   □ People you know whose feet take good tidings to "high places" (the hard and dangerous assignments).
   □ Those who are called to share the Gospel and are at low points in their lives (e.g., missionaries in situations where their lives are at risk).
   □ People whose feet have wandered off in the wrong direction (particularly young people).
   □ The direction your own feet are going (see Psalm 119:35).

5 minutes

3. (On your own) Complete the following prayer exercises:
   □ Retrace your own footsteps this past year. Is there anything you want to talk to the Lord about concerning them?
   □ Think of specific occasions in which spiritual leaders have helped you, and thank God for those people.
   □ Pray for people you know who are heading "home" (e.g., terminally ill friends or family).

5 minutes

4. Take a moment to share with a prayer partner your concerns about someone you love whose feet are not following the Lord. Then spend time praying for each other.

5 minutes

•DIGGING DEEPER•

In this lesson you will learn to do a topical Bible study using the principles outlined in *Opening the Book* by Hans Finzel. A topical study might be defined as "the method of tracing a specific subject through the Bible in order to summarize the Bible's teaching on that subject." Topical study can be done in one book, through several books, or throughout the entire Bible.'

The following step-by-step outline will guide you in doing a topical study on the *walk* of a Christian.

1. *Choose your topic of study.* For this study, our topic will be the Christian's *walk.*

2. *Collect all available information on your topic.* This can be done with the help of a concordance and a good study Bible. Look up the majority of references to your topic found in a Bible concordance. Also look up all relevant cross-references. Record your findings. For your study on the *walk* of the Christian, look up the following references to *walk* and make any notations you think are important.

Deuteronomy 5:33

Deuteronomy 10:12

Psalm 1:1

Psalm 15:2

Psalm 89:15

Isaiah 2:3

Isaiah 57:2

Jeremiah 6:16

Daniel 4:37

Micah 6:8

2 Corinthians 5:7

1 John 1:6

1 John 1:7

2 John 6

3. *Reflect on your findings.* Among the references you've looked up, what is the basic meaning of the word *walk?* (To determine the definition of *walk*, refer back to the instructions for doing a word study in the Digging Deeper section of chapter 1.)

4. *Organize your findings.* How are we to walk as believers in Christ?

   How are we not to walk?

5. *Consult study aids.* Compare your answer to question #3 with the *Theological Word Book of the Old Testament* and with *Vine's* word study on *walk* (listed below for your convenience). Did your conclusions agree with theirs?

   הָלַךְ (hālak) go, walk. ASV and RSV similar with the latter sometimes improving on the former.
   Our word denotes movement in general, although usually

of people. Hence, it can be applied with various connotations (including Josh 17:7), and in various contexts.

. . . The specific application of this verb to various kinds of going may be translated variously: e.g., the "creeping" of a snake (Gen 3:14), the "prowling" of foxes (Lam 5:18), the "sailing" of ships (Gen 7:18), the "flowing" of water (Gen 2:14), the "playing" of trumpets (Ex 19:19), the "walking" of men (Ex 14:19), etc. In another special use this verb signifies the end of, e.g., rain (Song 2:11), dew (Hos 6:4), wind (Ps 78:39), grief (Job 16:6), human life (Gen 15:2; Josh 23:14), etc.

This verb can be applied both to supposed gods (Ps 115:7) and to the Lord God. . . . Conceived anthropomorphically, God walks on the clouds (Ps 104:3) or in the heavens (Job 22:14). More frequently, and more importantly *hālak* is applied to Yahweh's coming to his people in judgment or blessing (2 Sam 7:23; Ps 80:2 [H 3]), especially during the wilderness wanderings (e.g., Ex 33:14; 13:21). In this latter context, note the new Exodus (Isa 45:2). As the people followed the ark of God through the desert so they followed it in ritual (infrequently expressed by *hālak;* cf. Josh 3:5; Num 10:32-36).

Apostasy is described as their "going after" other/false gods (Ex 32:1; Jer 5:23), pursuing one's own evil counsel (Jer 7:24; Ps 1:1), or heart (Jer 11:8), or walking in darkness (Isa 9:2 [H 1]), and meets with God's judgment (Lev 26:24). The truly pious follow God's leading in all that they do (i.e., they keep his commandments, 1 Kgs 3:14; Ps 119:1ff).[2]

WALK

I. PERIPATEO (περιπατέω) is used *(a)* physically, in the Synoptic Gospels (except Mark 7:5); always in the Acts except 21:21; never in the Pauline Epistles, nor in those of John; *(b)* figuratively, "signifying the whole round of the activities of the individual life, whether of the unregenerate, Eph. 4:17, or of the believer, 1 Cor. 7:17; Col. 2:6. It is applied to the observance of religious ordinances, Acts 21:21; Heb. 13:9, marg., as well as to moral conduct. The Christian is to walk in newness of life, Rom. 6:4, after the spirit, 8:4, in honesty, 13:13, by faith, 2 Cor. 5:7, in good works, Eph. 2:10, in love, 5:2, in wisdom, Col. 4:5, in truth, 2 John 4, after the commandments of the Lord, v. 6. And, negatively, not after the flesh, Rom. 8:4; not after the manner of men, 1 Cor. 3:3; not in craftiness, 2 Cor. 4:2; not by sight, 5:7; not in the vanity of the mind, Eph. 4:17; not disorderly, 2 Thess. 3:6.''³

Try to think of other words in Scripture that are similar in meaning to the word *walk*. Study these words or phrases by consulting a concordance and cross-referencing them. Then add these to your lists in questions #4 and #5.

6. *Choose the primary passage.* Look over all the passages you have studied to this point and select the one that seems to be the most significant.

   Reflect on the meaning of this passage. Assuming you selected 2 Corinthians 5:7 as your primary passage for the word *walk*, ask yourself, "What does it mean to 'walk by faith' "? (Go back and repeat steps 2 through 5 to answer this question.)

7. *State the teaching principles.* Make a list of all the principles you discovered for the topic you are studying (in this study it relates to the *walk* of a believer). Finzel suggests you do this by answering the question, "What does this topic have to say that is useful for Christian living and for the church in general?"⁴ These he calls the teaching principles. Mention at least four principles you found in your study on the *walk of a Christian*.

   1.

   2.

   3.

   4.

8. *Search the contexts and seek comparisons.* Consider your topic in light of what the rest of Scripture teaches. What other topics relate to the Christian's walk? Reflect on how other passages qualify or complement your subject.

9. *Consult secondary sources.* Refer to other study sources only after you have completed your own study of Scripture. What do Bible dictionaries, theologies, or commentaries contribute to your understanding of the subject?

10. *State your conclusions.* What is the main point of what you've learned? Write down your own conclusion in a concise summary statement.

11. *Apply what you've learned to your own life.* This is the final step in topical Bible study. Finzel suggests that to do this step you:

> Know yourself.
> Relate the topic to life.
> Meditate on the results.
> Practice your findings.

To assist you in relating the Scriptures to life, Finzel suggests that the Christian life be viewed as a series of new relationships . . .

WITH GOD
☐ A truth to rest in
☐ A command to obey
☐ A prayer to express
☐ A challenge to heed
☐ A promise to claim
☐ A fellowship to enjoy

WITH YOURSELF
☐ A thought or a word to examine
☐ An action to take
☐ An example to follow
☐ An error to avoid
☐ An attitude to change or guard against
☐ A priority to change

☐ A goal to strive for
☐ A personal value or standard to hold up
☐ A sin to forsake

WITH OTHERS (HOME, CHURCH, WORK, SCHOOL, SOCIETY, THE WORLD)

☐ A witness to share
☐ An encouragement to extend
☐ A service to do
☐ A forgiveness to ask
☐ A fellowship to nurture
☐ An exhortation to give
☐ A burden to bear
☐ A kindness to express
☐ A hospitality to extend
☐ An attitude to change or guard against
☐ A sin to forsake

WITH SATAN

☐ A piece of spiritual armor to wear
☐ A temptation to resist
☐ A device to recognize
☐ A person to resist
☐ A sin to avoid and confess[5]

For Further Study

1. Complete the study you began in question #5 on the meaning of the walk of faith.
2. Trace your own personal walk of faith throughout your Christian life.

•TOOL CHEST•
(A Suggested Optional Resource)

OPENING THE BOOK

The guidelines for the topical method of Bible study outlined in the Digging Deeper section of this chapter, are from *Opening the Book* by Hans Finzel (Victor Books, 1987). This companion volume to *Unlocking the Scriptures* is filled with a variety of Bible study methods which can be applied inductively to the different kinds of literature found within the sixty-six books of Scripture. That is exactly the genius of Finzel's second volume. It shows us step by step how to apply the inductive method of Bible study to every book of the Bible, whether it be narrative, poetry, didactic, or prophetic literature. He unveils the phrases for studying small and larger portions of Scripture within the context of the entire Bible.

7
Seeing Eyes

•FOOD FOR THOUGHT•

It is a terrible affliction to be blind! When torturers want to add to their victims' misery, they blindfold them. Jesus knew something of this, as we see in Mark 14:65, "They blindfolded [Jesus] and struck Him with their fists." Yet, if it is a terrible affliction to be physically blind, how much worse to be spiritually sightless.

Jesus told the Pharisees that they were "blind leaders of the blind" (Matt. 15:14). He, of course, was referring to their lack of spiritual understanding. He explained that men are born blind to God's will and purpose. Sin has robbed men of their spiritual sight. The Apostle Paul stated it this way: "The god of this age has blinded the minds of unbelievers, so that they cannot see the light of the Gospel of the glory of Christ, who is the image of God" (2 Cor. 4:4).

The spiritually blind are "lost." They grope about, looking for answers to life like blind men grope for something to hold on to. Jesus said He had come "to seek and to save that which was lost" (Luke 19:10). Because Jesus is the Light of the world, He can save us from our blindness. But the choice is ours. We can either choose to allow Him to illuminate our lives with His truth, asking Him to remove the cataracts of sin from our spiritual eyes, or we can reject His truth and remain spiritually blind.

Once enlightened, however, Christians still do at times suffer from spiritual eye disorders. Some believers, for instance, are thoroughly shortsighted. Physical shortsightedness can keep us from being effective and productive, and so can spiritual shortsightedness. If we see only the needs within our own church walls, then we're not likely to see the need for a worldwide church missions program or an effective youth outreach in the community.

Another spiritual eye disorder some Christians are afflicted with is farsightedness. Which of us hasn't had folk around us who are busy having "visions" but who are not very good at working them out using common sense? When you're farsighted, it's often difficult to see what's going on right under your own nose. In fact, you may be in danger of being so heavenly minded, you are no earthly good!

Some Christians may also suffer from spiritual double vision. Jesus said that if our eye is single it will be full of light. Being single-minded in our purpose to follow the Lord is the way to correct double vision. Jesus illustrated the need for single-mindedness when He told His disciples, "You cannot serve both God and money" (Luke 16:13).

It is extremely important that we deal drastically with any eye problems that occur. The Lord said, "If your eye causes you to sin, pluck it out" (Mark 9:47). He, of course, was speaking figuratively, but this in no way weakens His point. If David had dealt with his lazy eye, and Bathsheba had refused "eye contact" with the king, perhaps their story would have ended in a much less tragic way.

The Bible talks of having eyes full of adultery (2 Peter 2:14), and a look of lust, leading to the act of sin (Matt. 5:28). While the first look in itself isn't sin, the second one usually is! As an old Chinese proverb puts it, "You can't stop the birds from flying over head, but you can keep them from nesting in your hair." We need to make a covenant with our eyes—promising God that our eyes will be given to Him.

When I was a student, I had a great deal of trouble looking men straight in the eye. I had learned by copying my Hollywood idols to look coyly at members of the opposite sex, using my eyes to relay all sorts of messages. Even when I was with a boyfriend, I found that my eyes could be having a conversation with someone else across the room. But then I became a Christian, and I discovered in Scripture that Job had made "a covenant with his eyes not to look upon a maid" (Job 31:1). He decided he would be faithful to his marriage partner. So I made a promise too, even though I wasn't married. I very distinctly remember kneeling down and telling God He could have my eyes. And the promises I made to Him that day were ones that only He could help me keep.

Yes, there are any number of reasons why we might have trouble with our eyesight, not least of which is having something in the eye itself. All of us know how painful and debilitating it is to have even a small speck of dirt in our eyes. Jesus, drawing on this common experience of people living in the dusty Middle East, said, "How can you say to your brother, 'Let me take the speck out of your eye,' when all the time there is a plank in your own eye?" (Matt. 7:4) Criticism of others surely blinds us to our own faults. "Anoint your eyes with eye salve that you may see," advises Jesus (Rev. 3:18). How often we need Jesus' healing touch to correct our failing eyesight!

If it is true that we need to have "eyes in our heart" to see spiritual realities, then it is also true that we need to have "heart in our eyes" if we are going to respond to the needs we see. In Matthew 9:36 we read that when Jesus saw the crowds, "He was moved with compassion on them, because they fainted, and were scattered abroad, as sheep having no shepherd." The NIV describes the people Jesus saw that day in Galilee as "harrassed and helpless." These words were strong, describing a people who were "strung out, needing support." Do we, like Jesus, have "heart in our eyes" so that when we see people, wandering through life like sheep without a shepherd, strung out and needing support, we respond compassionately? If we see things His way, we will not be looking at life through rose-colored spectacles, but with the clear, caring look of love.

There is another reason why our vision may sometimes be impaired—tears! Do we cry so long and loud over our own misfortunes, that we fail to see the answer, which may well be close at hand? Hagar, dying of thirst in the desert and blinded by her own tears, did not see the well of water right in front of her that God used to save her life and that of her son, Ishmael (Gen. 21:15-19). Then there was Mary, who crying copiously at the Garden tomb, was so blinded by her own grief that she didn't even recognize Jesus when He was standing right in front of her (John 20:10-16). Mourning a loved one without allowing God to dry our tears can be a real problem. It's during times of deep distress such as this that we especially need to remember the comforting words of Scripture, words like, "For you, O Lord, have delivered my soul from death, my eyes from tears, and my feet from stumbling" (Ps. 116:8).

In ancient times, when mourners went to the grave to weep for their dead, they would often take a wineskin bottle with them and weep into it. Then they would leave their "grief" at the graveside. We see this graphic picture in Psalm 56:8 where the Psalmist David prayed to the Lord, "Put Thou my tears in Thy bottle." What comfort and joy to know that God is fully aware of my tears. In fact, I think He counts each tear carefully; He does not forget them! The Book of Revelation promises us that one day "*He* will wipe every tear from [our] eyes" (Rev. 21:4).

> Tears talking,
> pattering petition on the door of heaven—
> Let me in.

Wet misery,
    fountains of fury,
        rivers of recrimination—
tears tearing down the riverbed of doubt—
        stopping at the throne.
Bottled bereavement,
    arranged by angels,
        given to the King!
God tilts the bottle carefully over His book
    of remembrance,
        letting the drops fall onto a clean page.
Transported in a teardrop,
        translated into eloquence,
my washing woe writes its words of wounded
    worry down.
Splashing sadness signs its name;
    then dry depression comes to stay,
        for all the tears have gone.
The Father reads my tears,
    passes the book to the Son,
        who shares it with the Spirit.
The angels gather 'round.
    Some small celestial cherubs
        are lifted to the Father's knees:
            The story is told.
They listen.
        They all listen.
            I am heard!
"I have heard her prayers; I have seen her tears,"
        says the Father.
"I am touched with the feelings of her infirmities,"
        says the Son.
"I will pray for her with groanings which cannot be uttered,"
        says the Spirit.
"And God shall wipe all tears from her eyes,"
    sing the angels.
"And there shall be no more death
    Neither sorrow nor crying,
Neither shall there be any more pain,
    For the former things shall pass away!" "[1]

Do you need Jesus to open your eyes to your sinful state, your need of a Saviour, and your dangerous predicament? Or do you, as an enlightened believer who prides himself or herself on seeing spiritual realities, have eye problems because of a shortsighted theological viewpoint or farsighted idea based on unrealistic or impractical thinking? Maybe your eye problem is a plank in the eye that hasn't, unfortunately, kept you from seeing the speck in someone else's eye. Or perhaps it's just that you need the Lord to dry your tears so you can see Him by your side. Whatever the problem, the Eye Doctor knows just what you need.

Healthy eyes, belonging to spiritually healthy Christians, see "eye to eye" with God. Their physical eyes appreciate His beautiful universe while their spiritual eyes get a glimpse of His face and move them to worship. May we

"see Him more clearly,
love Him more dearly,
follow Him more nearly day by day!"[2]

•TALKING IT OVER•

---

1. READ AND DISCUSS.   *10 minutes*

Spiritual blindness.

☐ Read John 3:16-21. What do you learn about God in this passage? About some blind people? About some sighted people?

Spiritual light.

☐ What did you *see* spiritually when you first *saw* Jesus? Describe it. (Example: "I saw that I was not good enough for God or heaven.)

---

2. SHARE PERSONALLY.   *15 minutes*

Spiritual eye trouble.

☐ Which malady has affected your spiritual eyesight? (Circle one and explain.)

Cataracts	Double vision
Nearsightedness	Farsightedness
Planks	Tears

☐ Read 2 Peter 1:5-9. What keeps you from seeing things God's way?
☐ Once God has given you a "seeing" heart, you may find yourself crying tears of compassion. List:

3 Good Things About Tears	3 Bad Things About Tears

---

3. PRAY.   *5 minutes*

Pray about some of the spiritual realities the Holy Spirit has shown you in this chapter.

•PRAYING IT THROUGH•

*Suggested
Times*

---

1. Praise God for opening your eyes to the needs of your own heart and the Saviour who is the answer to those needs.

3 minutes

---

2. As a group, pray:
   □ About the harassed people who need help, that God would give you eyes to see their needs and respond in compassion.
   □ That the Lord of the harvest would thrust forth workers to meet the needs of a hurting world.
   □ (Silently) About whether or not *you* should be one of those workers.

5 minutes

---

3. (In twos) Share one thing you would like to *see* more clearly in your own life. (Example: "God, help me to see Your purpose in letting this bad thing happen in my life.") Also pray that God would give you a clear look at Himself midst all the confusion of your situation.

6 minutes

---

4. Silently meditate, *looking* into the face of God, and pray. Then read Psalm 139 and *see* the assurance of His love expressed for you there. Thank Him for what He has shown you.

6 minutes

•DIGGING DEEPER•

John 9
1. Thoughtfully read John 9, recording your initial impressions of the passage as you read.

2. What does verse 2 tell you about first-century Jewish theology regarding sickness and suffering?

   Why, according to Jesus, was this man born blind?

3. What is the work of God that Jesus is talking about in verse 4?

   Are you doing this work?

4. How does Jesus refer to Himself in verse 5?

   Using a concordance, do a word study on the word *light* in the Book of John. Follow the directions in the Tool Chest section of chapter 1. Record your findings on a separate sheet of paper. Then answer this question: What does Jesus mean when He says He is the Light of the world?

5. Look up the word *Siloam* in a Bible dictionary. Also locate Siloam on a map of Jerusalem. Jot down what you learn.

Keeping in mind the context of verse 7, why do you think John emphasized that "Siloam . . . means sent"?

What would it indicate about Jesus to those who read the Gospel of John in the first and second centuries?

Is this a common theme in the Book of John? (Check a concordance to answer this question.)

6. When his neighbors questioned him, to what did the blind man attribute his sight?

7. Why is the fact that Jesus healed the blind man on the Sabbath significant? (v. 14)

The following comments from F.F. Bruce's *The Gospel of John* will help you see how the Pharisees interpreted the keeping of the Sabbath.

So, Jesus had repeated the offense which led to so much trouble on the occasion of an earlier visit to Jerusalem: he had performed an act of healing on the sabbath. Not that an act of healing as such infringed the sabbath law, but an act of healing was very likely to involve something else which did infringe the law. On the former occasion Jesus encouraged a man to carry a burden through the streets on the sabbath; on this occasion he made a mud poultice with earth and saliva. What was wrong with that? Simply this: one of the categories of work specifically forbidden on the sabbath in the traditional interpretation of the law was kneading, and the making of mud or clay with such simple ingredients as earth and saliva was construed as a form of kneading.[3]

Based on Matthew 12:1-14 and Mark 2:23-28, what do you think Jesus interpreted keeping the Sabbath to mean?

What Old Testament example does He give to support His argument?

According to Jesus, what was the intended purpose of the Sabbath?

8. What response would you have expected this miracle to prompt in the hearts of religious men?

The Book of Isaiah contains many messianic prophecies which foretell the coming of Christ. What would the Pharisees have expected of God's Anointed One, had they really understood these passages?

Isaiah 29:17-18

Isaiah 35:5

Isaiah 42:7

Instead, the Pharisees were divided in their reaction to this marvelous miracle. What assumption did some of them make? (John 9:16a)

What conclusion did the others come to and why? (v. 16b)

9. Why did the man's parents respond as they did to the Pharisees' questions? (v. 23)

What would being excommunicated from the synagogue have meant in practical terms to his parents?

10. What were the Pharisees implying when they demanded, "Give glory to God"? (v. 24)

The former blind man gave his testimony in response to their demands, "I was blind but now I see!" (v. 25) In doing this he certainly did give glory to God! What is your testimony of the work of God in your life?

11. How were the Pharisees' claims to be disciples of Moses supposed to defend their credibility?

Why is this invalid in light of Hebrews 1:1-2 and 3:3-6?

12. To the man's profound defense of Jesus Christ, the Pharisees replied with this cruel retort, "You were steeped in sin at birth" (v. 34). Read the following excerpt from *Handbook of Life in Bible Times,* and then in your own words, write a possible explanation for their accusation.

PHYSICAL DISABILITY
Eye diseases caused by climatic factors, infection, venereal disease, and the effects of heredity or senility were common in Bible times. Total blindness occurred in newborn infants (Jesus healed a man blind from birth), and this may have been a severe conjunctivitis which results from venereal infection. (If so, that would have given a double edge to the Pharisees' rejection of the man as 'steeped in sin at birth'.[4]

13. From what you read in verses 35-38 of John 9, how would you characterize this man's spiritual condition?

14. What does Jesus permit in verse 38 that the following verses would otherwise seem to prohibit?

Isaiah 42:8

Isaiah 43:10-11

Isaiah 44:6

Revelation 22:8-9

What, then, does this passage reveal about Jesus' identity?

15. How can we reconcile verse 39 of John 9 with John 3:17 and 12:27?

Jesus Christ was then, and is now, a point of division. Has your belief in Him caused division among your family, friends, or colleagues?

16. What did the man who was blind recognize in Jesus and acknowledge that the Pharisees did not?

What is the penalty for claiming to see yet disbelieving and rejecting that Jesus Christ is from God? (vv. 39-41)

Do you ever claim to know something which you really do not, or to be someone you really are not, or to be more spiritual than you really are? Take a moment to reflect on this question and confess your spiritual blindness to the Lord.

17. In what ways is John 9 an illustration of Jesus' statement, "I am the Light of the world"? (v. 5)

What have you learned about Him from your study of this chapter?

Write down the response He desires from you as a result of what you now know.

18. Ask the Lord Jesus to open your spiritual eyes in order that you may understand more fully who He is.

For Further Study

1. Do a concordance study on the "I am" statements of Jesus in the Gospel of John.
2. Trace the Pharisees' response to Jesus through the Gospel of John.

·TOOL CHEST·
(A Suggested Optional Resource)

HANDBOOK OF LIFE IN BIBLE TIMES
Longing to visit the Holy Land? Colorful, picture-filled, and graphi-
cally illustated, the *Handbook of Life in Bible Times* will make you feel as
though you were really there. This study companion to the Bible will
introduce you to the history and culture of Bible times in such detail
that you may think you could write a sketch for the *U.S. Background
Notes* on Israel! Some of the subjects which are covered in this
attractive textbook are *industry, commerce, culture, health, warfare, religion,
domestic affairs*, and much more. Helpful indexes will assist you in
turning quickly to pertinent information for preparing messages and
Bible studies as well as for your own personal enrichment. This study
volume is published by InterVarsity Press and can be purchased from
your local Christian bookstore for $34.95.

8

Listening Ears

•FOOD FOR THOUGHT•

It seems that the world around us has one great big hurting heart! And this needy world is just waiting for someone to listen. Hurting hearts need a hearing, and hearing necessitates listening ears.

The poet Seneca, a Roman philosopher who died by his own hand at the order of the Emperor Nero, said in his final hours, "Listen to me for a day, for an hour, a moment, lest I expire in my terrible wilderness, my lonely silence. Oh God! Is there no one to listen?"¹ When there is no one to listen, a terrible sense of isolation pervades one's soul. But when we can share our troubles and someone listens, we feel we are no longer alone. The truth is—a trouble shared is a trouble halved!

Listening alone is not enough—one must listen with love. On a tour of the mission field in Africa, my husband, who was the invited Bible teacher, found that his "outside" ears were "bent" on a pretty continuous basis, as were mine. And what *I* learned is that the ministry of listening is just as important as the ministry of lecturing. In fact, at one point on that tour a young teenager wrote me a note, thanking me for listening. She ended her note by saying, "Because you listened to me, I listened to you." Ah—now there's a big lesson to learn—listen first; speak last! Many times we have to earn the right to speak by listening first.

I also discovered that if you really love, you will really listen. Love always listens to the other person because true love is primarily concerned with the other's well-being, irrespective of the cost to itself. To love God first, others next, and yourself last will indeed ensure you as a good listener.

God has called us to listen. Jesus said on numerous occasions, "He who has ears, let him hear" (Matt. 11:15). Also, divine revelation depends on our *hearing* a message from God, as Hebrews 1:1-2 tells us: "In the past God spoke to our forefathers through the prophets at many times and in various ways, but in these last days He has spoken to us by His Son." One day as Jesus was busy about His earthly ministry, God the Father put His stamp of approval on His Son when He leaned out of heaven and said, "This is My beloved Son . . . *hear ye Him*" (Matt. 17:5). Notice, He did not say, "This is My beloved Son . . . talk His ear off!" If faith comes by hearing, and hearing by the Word of God, then we'd better begin to listen if we are going to be people of faith.

Samuel was a great man of faith. As prophet, his job was to listen to God's message and relay it to the people. As priest, he listened to the people and relayed their messages to God! And in the New Testament, we read about the *priest*hood of believers (Rev. 1:4-6), which means, therefore, that Christians' ears are *called* and *commissioned* to care. They are "captive" ears.

In Bible times, when an opportunity came about for a slave to be set free, that slave could choose to say, "I love my master and will not go out free." If he did this, then the master would take that slave to a doorpost and pierce his ear with an awl. From that time on, the slave was a "marked man." There was absolutely no doubt how that slave felt about his master!

So it should be with Christians. People should know whose we are and whom we serve by our listening, loving ears. Pardoned ears are "pierced ears," which bear an unmistakable message to the world: "We will listen to and obey our beloved Master." Perhaps each time we put in our earrings we should remember that!

There's another valuable lesson we need to learn about listening: listening does not demand a verbal response. We don't *have* to say something whenever we're listening to someone's troubles. There *is* such a thing as a "ministry of presence." Silence is, for some of us more than others, a learned art. Listening is a matter of control and concentration.

I remember one occasion when Stuart had to travel abroad for three months. Finally, the long-awaited day of his return came and I took the children down to the airport to meet their dad. All four of us were bursting with things to tell him—it was about 3 months x 4 people's worth! Poor Stuart! For the whole of the two-and-a-half hour trip back home, the kids and I poured our words all over him. Having just made a rather lengthy flight across the Atlantic, he was understandably sleepy, but he tried valiantly to stay awake and listen. As we drove into the driveway, just about talked out, he said in a quiet voice, "I had a nice time too." Not one of us had taken time to listen to *him*. Listening is definitely a matter of control!

Another thing to remember about listening is that it requires some very important body language. We have to *look* as though we are listening. And how do we do this? First, we do it by looking the person we are listening to straight in the eyes, as if to say, "Come on, let's have it. You have my undivided attention." This is true even when the one we are listening to is a small child. We need to bend down and be at the child's level when he or she has something to tell us. People will find it hard to believe that we are listening to them if our eyes are constantly moving beyond them while they are talking, or if we are glancing at the clock or our wristwatch. They are likely to get the message that we would like them to hurry up and finish so we can get on with more important things. They certainly will not be inclined to open up to us. And who can blame them? If we will but learn to listen without hurry, we will be saying to the hurting person, "You matter more to me than my schedule."

A second thing to remember about listening is that it comes with maturity. Self-centered people are rarely good listeners. Christ-centered people are. Women have a tendency to be poor listeners, perhaps because they generally love to talk! In fact, an endless number of jokes have been told on the subject. You've probably heard some. I know, for myself, that I love to complete my husband's sentences for him, a fact that irritates him considerably. Also, self-centered people usually listen to others with an ulterior motive, as this little poem points out.

I lend a sympathetic ear
to other people's woes.
However dull it is to hear
their real or fancied throes.
I pay to every gloomy line attention undiminished,
because I plan to start on mine
the moment that they've finished!

If we aspire to be good listeners, we are going to have to abandon our preoccupation with self.

Third, good listeners will be much in prayer. In Isaiah 50:4 we read, "The Sovereign Lord has given me an instructed tongue, to know the word that sustains the weary. He wakens me morning by morning, wakens my ear to listen like one being taught." I have written in my Bible by the side of that verse, "Get up and listen to Me so you can go out and listen to them." Even the finest listener in

100

the world cannot meet the needs of a soul. Only God can do that. So I'd better stay long enough at my bedside, listening to Him, if I hope to answer from His perspective the questions I am going to be asked during the course of my day. There's a big difference between our own advice—however clever we think we are—and God's wisdom. We need to depend on the Holy Spirit to help us listen without lecturing; quit being so quick to offer an opinion on everything; stop using Scripture as an instant fix; and refrain from giving out advice so freely.

Some problems, of course, have no easy answers, and we must not try and manufacture any. What we *can* do, is simply be there to let the hurting one know he or she can count on us, listening with love and loving to listen until the storm has passed.

Being good listeners, at times, may mean offering a well-placed word of advice. One of the hazards of doing this, however, is that the hurting party may, in the end, reject your advice. Try not to take it personally. Just remember what the Lord told Samuel, "It is not you they have rejected, but they have rejected Me" (1 Sam. 8:7). We are often tempted to think in such situations that because they have rejected our advice, they have rejected us! Not so. Say what you have to say with love and try to take the people to the Scriptures for their answers, keeping the relationship open, if possible. Then leave the rest in God's hands. When you finally get to glory, you can tell the Lord all about it, face to face. And be assured, you'll find a listening ear and an appreciative Saviour, waiting there to hear *your* side of the story.

A missionary friend once told me about an experience she and her husband had had upon returning from the mission field after more than thirty years of service. They had served the Lord in such an isolated region of the world. Trips back home had been few and far between. "We had twenty years of news to share," she confided in me, "and we couldn't wait to get started." Imagine this couple's disappointment when the boat finally docked and they realized that nobody was there to meet them. No one to give them a hug. No one to help carry thirty years' worth of goods and clothes ashore. And worst of all, no one to listen!

As my friends stood on the dock holding onto only each other, they said to the Lord, "We're home and no one cares!" Then the Lord seemed to whisper to their hurting hearts, "Oh, but you're not *home* yet!" When we grow weary, hoping to find someone to listen, remember, "We're not home yet!" One day we shall be and we'll be heard out. Until then, why not lend your ears to a hurting world and discover a ministry beyond your wildest dreams?

•TALKING IT OVER•

1. LISTEN TO GOD.   *10 minutes*
   ☐ Read 1 Samuel 1–2 as a group. What do you
     learn about . . .
     Elkanah?
     Peninnah?
     Hannah?
     Eli?
   ☐ What is *one* lesson about listening each of these   *10 minutes*
     people teaches us?

2. LISTEN TO EACH OTHER.   *10 minutes*
   (In twos) Each of you, spend 3 minutes sharing
   with your partner a hurt you've experienced. The
   person who is listening should try to think of a
   verse from Scripture (i.e., an illustration, a word of
   encouragement or comfort, a piece of advice, etc.)
   that has helped in a similar situation and share it
   with the other person. Close by praying for each
   other's needs.

• PRAYING IT THROUGH •

Suggested Times

1. Thank the Lord for:

   □ Your ears. Think of all the things you hear with them that you would like to thank God for; then thank Him for those things.

   □ A few of the things you have heard in church or from spiritual teachers that have changed your life. Be specific.

5 minutes

2. Pray for:

   □ People who are physically deaf *and* for those who minister spiritually to them.

   □ Those who are spiritually deaf to God's voice, that they would *hear* the voice of the Holy Spirit.

   □ Your own ministry as a listener.

8 minutes

3. (On your own) Take a moment now to *listen* to the Holy Spirit. What has He said to you through today's lesson? Respond to Him. Spend a few minutes memorizing Isaiah 50:4 as you wrap up this time of personal reflection.

7 minutes

•DIGGING DEEPER•

1. Read these verses within their contexts (in relationship to the verses which both precede and follow them), and write down what the Bible has to say about listening.

   Deuteronomy 30:20

   1 Samuel 3:9

   Nehemiah 8:3

   Proverbs 1:5

   Proverbs 12:15

   Proverbs 18:13

   Ecclesiastes 5:1

   Isaiah 66:4

   Daniel 9:6

   Mark 9:7

   Luke 10:39

   John 10:27

   James 1:19

   James 1:22

   1 John 4:6

2. What are some synonyms for the word *listen?* Choose one or two that are significant and look these words up in a concordance. Write down at the top of the next page any references and additional information you find which adds new insight to your understanding of the biblical concept of listening.

3. Mull over the information you have collected. What is the basic meaning of the word *listen* which is common to all the occurrences of it in Scripture?

4. Categorize your findings under major concepts or headings (i.e., To Whom We Are to Listen; Benefits of Listening; Consequences of Not Listening, etc.).

5. Read the following excerpts from *The New International Dictionary of New Testament Theology*. What do these add to your knowledge of listening?

Hear, Obey
The word hear embraces both physical hearing and the apprehension of something with the mind.

The linguistic and conceptual relationship between *akouō* and *hypakouō* recurs in Old and Middle Eng. in the use of the same word for both hear and obey.

In biblical revelation hearing has a much greater significance than in the Gk. or Hel. worlds. For God meets man in his word, and man therefore is charged with hearing God's word.

God lets his judgment fall on a people that will not hear; nor is he any longer willing to hear this people (Isa. 1:15; cf. Ezek. 8:18).

enōtizomai, pay attention to, hear, is derived from *ous*, ear. . . . Thus the OT contains a whole range of statements in which the pious Israelite expressed his certainty that God hears and answers prayer. It is put particularly beautifully in Ps. 94:9: "He who planted the ear, does he not hear?" On the other hand, man's guilt can step between God and man and make God's ear deaf, so that he does not hear (Isa. 59:1 f.).[1]

6. Of all the verses you have studied, which would you select as the key passage (providing you with the most valuable insight) on listening?

7. What biblical principles have you discovered in regard to listening?

8. What/whom will you listen to this week?

   How will you demonstrate that you have indeed heard?

   What/whom will you try to avoid listening to this week?

9. Review the eight Digging Deeper sections in this book. What personal lessons has God taught you about Himself, your own body language, the Bible, faith, etc.?

10. Write a prayer to your Heavenly Father, praising Him for who He is and what He has taught you. Confess your need to listen to Him more unreservedly, and ask Him to help you to hear Him when He speaks to you.

•TOOL CHEST•
(A Suggested Optional Resource)

THE NEW INTERNATIONAL DICTIONARY
OF NEW TESTAMENT THEOLOGY
This three-volume, hardback, New Testament Theology is for the experienced Bible student. It provides in-depth, critical discussions of significant themes and words in the New Testament without isolating concepts from their Old Testament counterparts. Topics are listed in English by alphabetical order. Hebrew and Greek equivalents are given and defined with scriptural examples. Usages of the word in other ancient literature are discussed along with various cognates of the word. Though *The New International Dictionary of New Testament Theology* is a rather expensive reference work, many times you can purchase it at a discount price through book clubs, such as Christian Book Distributors and Scripture Truth Book Company. Colin Brown is the editor of this reference work and Zondervan, the publisher.

•NOTES•

Chapter 1: Presenting Our Bodies
[1]Hal Boyle, *Quotable Quotations* (Wheaton: Victor Books, 1985), p. 362.
[2]C.E.B. Cranfield, *A Critical and Exegetical Commentary on the Epistle to the Romans*, *Vol. II, ICC* (Edinburgh: T & T Clark, 1979), p. 597.
[3]William Morris, ed., *The American Heritage Dictionary of the English Language* (Boston: Houghton Mifflin Company, 1976), p. 470.

Chapter 2: Transforming Our Minds
[1]Source unknown.
[2]"Oh Jesus, I Have Promised," words by John E. Bode, from *Hymns for the Living Church* (Carol Stream: Hope Publishing Company, 1974), p. 506.
[3]Jill Briscoe, *There's a Snake in My Garden* (Grand Rapids: Zondervan, 1975), p. 28.
[4]Alfred Marshall, *The New International Version Interlinear Greek-English New Testament* (Grand Rapids: Zondervan, 1976), pp. 640-641.

Chapter 3: Changing Our Hearts
[1]F.B. Meyer, *David* (Fort Washington: Christian Literature Crusade, 1977), p. 199.

Chapter 4: Taming Our Tongues
[1]Hans Finzel, *Unlocking the Scriptures* (Wheaton: Victor Books, 1986), pp. 46-47.

Chapter 5: Helping Hands
[1]W.E. Vine, *An Expository Dictionary of New Testament Words* (New Jersey: Fleming H. Revell Company, 1966), p. 265.
[2]Kenneth S. Wuest, *Word Studies in the Greek New Testament, Volume 1* (Grand Rapids: Wm. B. Eerdmans, 1973), pp. 59-60.

Chapter 6: Fitting Our Feet
[1]Hans Finzel, *Opening the Book* (Wheaton: Victor Books, 1987), p. 275.
[2]R. Laird Harris, Gleason L. Archer, and Bruce K. Waltke, *Theological Wordbook of the Old Testament, Vol. I* (Chicago: Moody Press, 1980), p. 216.
[3]W.E. Vine, *An Expository Dictionary of New Testament Words* (New Jersey: Fleming H. Revell Company, 1966), pp. 1217-1218.
[4]*Opening the Book*, p. 289.
[5]Ibid., pp. 347-348.

Chapter 7: Seeing Eyes
[1]Jill Briscoe, *Fight for the Family* (Grand Rapids: Zondervan, 1981), pp. 45-46.
[2]"Day by Day," words by St. Richard of Chichester, © Word Music, 1986.
[3]F.F. Bruce, *The Gospel of John* (Grand Rapids: Wm. B. Eerdmans, 1983), p. 212.
[4]J.A. Thompson, *Handbook of Life in Bible Times* (Downers Grove: InterVarsity Press, 1986), p. 271.

Chapter 8: Listening Ears
[1]Colin Brown, editor, *The New International Dictionary of New Testament Theology, Vol. 2* (Grand Rapids: Zondervan, 1976), pp. 172-180.